The Value of a I

Isabel C. Byrum

Alpha Editions

This edition published in 2024

ISBN : 9789362926654

Design and Setting By
Alpha Editions
www.alphaedis.com
Email - info@alphaedis.com

Contents

PREFACE.

This book has a purpose: it is sent forth as precious seed, with the prayer that it will fall into "good soil" in many hearts and bring forth an hundredfold.

All parents with natural affection desire the best things for their children. Such fathers and mothers have high hopes that from their home will go forth noble men and women—yes, even heroes. Many fail to realize the attainment of this ideal in their children, because of a lack of the knowledge necessary to bring about the desired development in the child-life.

The following pages were written with the fervent hope that they would, at least in some measure, be a help in developing the young lives entrusted to your care. If your harvest-time is past; if your children have grown up and have left the old home, you may be able to help some one who still has little ones to train.

One object in relating actual experiences was that the reader might be guided in the application of those principles of child-training which, if merely stated in the abstract, might be hard to understand and difficult of application. The principles herein stated are not mere theories, but they have the commendation of having stood the test of use. Two other objects of this simple story of home life are that the thoughtful mother may get a view of the effects of certain extreme environments on the child-life and, by observing the substantial results accomplished by a praying mother, she may discover the secret of success.

The incidents of this little home story are all true, even to minute details, as far as memory serves one of the actors in this drama of home life after the lapse of many years; but as most of the principal characters are still living, the correct names have, for the most part, been withheld. Should one of your children ask, "Mama, who was Bessie Worthington?" you can truthfully answer, "She was a little girl who lived in Michigan; and she and her papa and mama are still living."

If, by reading this little book, any mother shall see wherein she can improve upon her past teaching, and thus be able to do more for the spiritual and moral well-being of her children, the writer will feel amply rewarded. May the blessing of God attend it as it goes forth.

Yours in Him,

Isabel C. Byrum.

CHAPTER I.

TWO SCENES.

How delightful to step into the home where God is counselor of both parent and child! How blessed the companionship in such a home! There God counsels in sweet, tender tones. He teaches his will and gives the needed wisdom. God is man's truest and best teacher. James says, "If any of you lack wisdom, let him ask of God, that giveth to all men liberally ... and it shall be given him." Be the home ever so beautiful, if it is not a house of prayer, it is not a place of true happiness. Parents should often commune with the Lord; especially the mother, with her many cares and perplexities, if she would do justice to the little ones entrusted to her care.

A beautiful picture now comes to my mind—a picture of an ideal mother of olden time. She dwelt in Ramah of Palestine. Her lonely home nestled among the lonely hills. She loved to commune with the Lord, for deep in her bosom she carried a sorrow that only he could help her to bear. Her home lacked that sweet sunlight which innocent childhood brings. She longed and prayed for a little life to guide and direct in the ways of the Lord.

Once every year she went with her husband to Shiloh, where sacrifices were offered, and there publicly worshiped the Lord. When at the house of the Lord one day, she prayed long and earnestly that God would grant the desire of her heart. "O Lord of hosts," she prayed, "if thou wilt indeed look on the affliction of thine handmaid, and remember me, and not forget thine handmaid, but wilt give unto thine handmaid a man child, then I will give him unto the Lord all the days of his life, and there shall no razor come upon his head."

A scene like this must have been rare even to the priest of God; for he mistook this sad woman for one drunken with wine. She begged him not to look upon her as such. When the man of God saw by her modest, earnest words that she was not drunken as he had supposed, he changed his reproof into a blessing. "Go in peace," he said, "and the God of Israel grant thy petition that thou hast asked of him." With perfect confidence that God had heard and answered prayer, the woman arose and returned with her husband to their home in Ramah.

The next year she did not go up to Shiloh; for God had granted her petition and had given her a little son. Her husband was willing for her to remain at home, but he cautioned her not to forget her promise to the Lord. He feared, perhaps, that the mother might become so attached to her child that she would be unwilling to part with him as she had promised. His warning was unnecessary.

As soon as Samuel (for this is what the mother named her son) was old enough to be useful, she took him to the house of God and presented him to the Lord. It must have sounded to the aged priest (who soon would have to cease his work upon earth) like a voice from heaven, when the happy mother, pointing to her child, said: "For this child I prayed; and the Lord hath given me my petition which I asked of him: therefore also I have lent him to the Lord; as long as he liveth he shall be lent to the Lord."

Again the mother prays; this time not in sorrow, but from a heart filled with thanksgiving. She feels no regret because of her vow. Her child became a great blessing to many people, and the Lord gave her other sons and daughters to cheer her heart.

By reading the story we find that "the child Samuel grew and was in favor both with the Lord and also with men." Why was this? In answer to his devoted mother's prayer, the Holy Spirit hovered over that child, shielding him from the cruel darts and arrows of the enemy. He had been taught the ways of the Lord from his cradle and his life was fully consecrated to God.

A different scene comes before me now—a scene that brings a shudder. Upon a ship sailing along the shores of France were a man and his wife on their way to join a band of villainous people in India. Being on a secret mission, they traveled slowly and carefully. It was a tedious and dangerous journey. One stormy day, on the Bay of Biscay, a child was born to them.

No loving welcome from the lips of a prayerful parent awaited this poor little innocent child; instead, curses were his portion, and, by the order of his mother, he was cast aside in a pile of rubbish to die. By chance the father passed that way and, finding his child's poor little perishing form, picked it up, took it to his wife, and commanded her to see that it was cared for.

As the child grew and developed in this atmosphere of sin and degradation, is it strange that he partook of his parents' nature and developed even worse habits than they? Unless the proper home influence is thrown around a child, he can not help suffering from the inherited sins of his parents.

When this child became a man, he knew nothing of virtue and honesty. His life was enveloped in a shroud of darkest crimes. Leaving India, he went to Europe and from there sailed to America. Each year found him better acquainted with court proceedings and prison walls. It was a common thing for him to break into a man's house and steal every valuable that he could find.

I recently met this man and heard from his own lips the dark story of his life. As he was relating an account of a desperate burglary, I asked him what he would have done if the man of the house had awakened. "Please do not ask me." he answered. "I was always armed, and a man's life was no more to me than a dog's. There are scenes that I can not, I dare not, recall, for I am a changed man now."

Thank God, he is a changed man. He had not been too vile for God to find. Jesus had cleansed his heart from all desire to do evil. Having confessed his crimes and given himself up to be punished, he had been sent to prison, but because of good behavior had been soon pardoned. He is now spending his life among the lower class, whom he understands so well and pities so much, trying to show them the way of salvation.

Note the atmosphere that surrounded the cradle of each of the babes of whom we have been speaking. In the first home we find prayer, love, hope, and tenderness; in the last, sin, hatred, crime, and villainy. Oh that mothers everywhere would take warning! If only these two pictures could be framed and hung in the recesses of every mother's heart where they might teach their silent lesson! If only mothers might see how powerful for good or evil is their influence; how the affections and the mental powers may be moulded by prayer and maternal love, and how the groundwork for the future of the child may be laid in its early training!

A sensible mother has a charm and wields an influence that takes a fast hold on the hearts of those who are dear to her. The kindly sympathy of youth, the deep affection of manhood, can be traced to influences that began at mother's knee.

What true, prayerful mother does not feel as her child closely nestles to her bosom that she is invested with a divine, mysterious power, an influence which she can not understand? Then it is that she sees her imperfections and longs for wisdom to know how to guide her child. God alone can supply that understanding. She is her child's book of wisdom, love, and, beauty, but she should be of God's writing.

CHAPTER II.

A PRAYING MOTHER.

Still another mother comes before my mind—an earnest, zealous, pious mother, who fashioned her life and example continually by God's Word and endeavored daily to teach her children the deep truths of salvation in language so simple that they could understand, to seek out the causes of their failures and discouragements, and to give them timely advice and instruction.

As I trace a few of her experiences, which are all true incidents, I trust they may sink into some perplexed mother's heart and enable her to wield the instruments of love and prayer about her darlings and to be more able to guide their tender hearts in the right course.

Mrs. Worthington lived in the great city of Chicago, in a small cottage on Portland Avenue near Thirty-first Street. Nothing about the dwelling was elaborate; everything was simple, but very neat. Pretty vines trailed gracefully over the porch and windows, and a few flower beds filled up the dull nooks and corners. In front of the house was a grassy lawn enclosed by a picket fence. Here the children could play apart from the rough waifs that thronged the street. Within the cottage the same quiet taste was in evidence.

Every day in her cozy sitting-room Mrs. Worthington talked with her little girls, Bessie and Louise. In times of trouble and perplexity she bowed with them in prayer. How much the children enjoyed their mother's comradeship and counsel! The mother realized the importance of these early impressions made on the child's mind. She had promised God to do all in her power to train her children for heaven. She had commenced early, even from the time she had first looked into the depths of their innocent eyes.

She had taught them that when any trouble arose between them, they were to kneel in prayer and ask God to help the one who had done wrong. Once she heard Bessie say, "Louise, I have prayed for you three times, and I believe I shall have to pray for you again." Louise was not a bad child; she had as sweet and happy a disposition as Bessie; but, as with all small children, little difficulties arose between them.

Wishing to know what her two little girls would do on such an occasion, she watched them. Bessie quietly took her little sister's hand, lead her aside, and knelt with her in prayer. Then with all earnestness she prayed, "O Lord, help Louise to to be good, for Jesus' sake. Amen." The prayer, though short, was effectual; for both went back to their play with happy faces, and they had no more trouble that day.

CHAPTER III.

EARLY TRAINING.

As the daily teaching continued, Mrs. Worthington taught her children many helpful lessons. She told them of the great necessity of a Savior and of his mission to humanity. She taught them how God looked upon disobedience, and always illustrated her talks with interesting Bible stories and their every-day experiences. In this way she taught them not only the evil effects of wrong-doing but also the sure reward of right-doing.

One summer, while the family was spending their vacation in Michigan at the pretty country home of an aunt, something happened that helped the children to apprehend their mother's meaning. This incident, although in some measure painful to Mrs. Worthington, impressed the lesson upon their young minds almost better than anything else could have.

The house was situated upon a hill that sloped gradually down to the shore of a lake. In many ways this lake was very attractive, especially to the two little girls, who were then at the ages of two and four years. Mrs. Worthington carefully warned the children of the danger of playing near the lake shore; but, not realizing the greatness of their temptation, she trusted them too far. Time after time they made their way down to the water's edge. Something must be done; but what?

One morning Mr. Worthington noticed his little daughters standing in front of the house. Although he could not hear their words, he clearly perceived that they were talking about a trip to the forbidden lake. They hesitated some time, but at last walked slowly down the hillside to the lake. Again they hesitated. Finally descending the steps of the boat-house, they stepped into the sparkling water. How dainty the ripples about their feet, and how clear the water!

"Surely there can be no harm or danger," thought Bessie; but she remembered the oft-repeated warnings of her parents and aunt. The shells lost their beauty when she remembered hearing her father say that bears sometimes travel up and down the shores. What if a bear should some that morning? She gave a quick, searching glance among the trees, but, seeing nothing, she tried to forget about bears. She might have been able to forget about them, but she could not forget that she was disobedient. Her conscience would not let her; the more she tried to forget, the louder it talked. She was just about to take her little sister back to the house, when she heard a rustling among the branches of a tall tree directly above the path over which she must pass. The next moment she thought she heard a low growl. "O

Louise," she cried, "I do believe that is the bear papa told us about." The tree then began to sway from side to side and they heard another growl, louder than the first. Seizing her little sister's hand, Bessie hastened to help her out of the water. By this time both were thoroughly frightened; for while visiting one of the parks in Chicago once, they had seen a bear hug his keeper until he could not stand. Bessie remembered the incident and tried to help Louise to hurry; but when the tree shook again, this time just above her, she screamed wildly and ran a few steps alone. When she got past the danger-point her reason returned, and, looking back, she saw her sister's great danger, as she stood just beneath the fatal tree. Rushing back, she almost carried Louise (while the growling continued), and they were soon up the hill. In the house they told of their strange experience, the substance of the story being, "The bear; The bear!"

Mr. Worthington soon joined the excited circle and secretly explained to his wife that he had been the supposed bear and that he had taken this course to teach the children a lesson. His plan was successful, for after that the children did not care to go to the lake alone.

Mrs. Worthington, however, was very sad because her children had been deceived. Unlike her husband, who was not a Christian, she believed in keeping the confidence of her children and in praying with them when they were disobedient. She decided to be more prompt and watchful in the future and to shield them from temptation as much as possible.

She improved the opportunity for some wholesome instruction. From the stories of Jonah and King Saul she brought forth some excellent lessons on disobedience. She told the children that, although they might think when tempted to disobey that nobody saw them, yet there was one whose eye was ever beholding their deeds, whether good or bad. Then she knelt in prayer with her children, praying with a full heart to that God who is everywhere present and from whom all our strength must come, that he would teach her how to guide the precious souls entrusted to her care.

CHAPTER IV.

GOD'S CARE.

Considering this mother's deep piety, do you think it strange that she saw God's hand in everything that befell her, and ascribed praise to him for it all?

After the return of the family to their home in Chicago the father became very ill. His sickness was so severe and so long continued that poverty began to threaten them. Mr. Worthington could not take the resigned view of their circumstances that his wife took, but often gave way to complaining. But Mrs. Worthington thanked God that things were no worse and ever encouraged her husband with the promises that God would provide.

At last Christmas morning came and found them in extreme poverty. Mr. Worthington still weak from his illness, but able to go around a little, came in from his morning walk very gloomy and feeling that his friends were very few. "This is the saddest Christmas I have ever known," he said to Mrs. Worthington. "It is almost more than I can bear to know that I have nothing to give the children today, and barely enough in the house to eat. I did not realize it so keenly until I saw an old man trudging along Thirty-first Street with a large pack upon his back. That man was surely going to surprise some of his friends. How much we need a friend like that!" "Never mind," said Mrs. Worthington softly; "God has promised to be a friend in time of need, and I believe he will care for us today."

As she finished speaking, a rap was heard at the door. Mr. Worthington arose slowly, wondering who could be their early caller. When he opened the door, he was greatly surprised to see the aged man with the pack and to find him to be his own father. Mr. Worthington had entered the house too soon to see his father turn the corner and enter the yard.

As the large burden was laid upon the floor and unpacked, there seemed to be no end to the good things. A turkey, cake, pies, in fact, all that was needful for a generous Christmas dinner, as well as a gift for each one. It was a very thankful family that gathered around the table that day.

CHAPTER V.

CONSECRATION.

In regard to her children, Mrs. Worthington had passed through a deep consecration. She fully realized that they were only lent her by the Lord, entrusted to her care to be trained for usefulness in his service, and she was determined to do all in her power to prepare them as the Lord intended. In all sincerity, she had placed her children upon the altar of consecration, promising God never to let her will interfere with his designs concerning them.

I do not think a child of God ever makes a consecration that is not tested in some form or other. This mother's consecration was tested.

A wealthy aunt, having lost all her children and being very lonely, thought to fill the vacancy in her heart and home by adopting a little child. After several vain attempts to find a suitable child, she sought the home of her niece, Mrs. Worthington. She came with many misgivings. When she made her errand known, her niece said: "Auntie, my children are no longer mine; I have given them to the Lord, and whatever is his will concerning them shall be mine. You will have to obtain my husband's consent." Thus far Aunt A. was delighted with her success, and she eagerly sought the father. She tried to point out to Mrs. Worthington, who was heartbroken at the prospect of losing her child, how abundantly able she (the aunt) was to provide for the child and spoke of the extreme poverty of the Worthington home. The mother knew all this, but she knew too that God's Spirit does not always rule in wealthy homes. Would she do right to let her child slip from under her parental care? Many thoughts of this nature surged through her brain, and many temptations to say no came to her; but instead of giving a decisive answer she sought counsel from the all-wise Counselor. While in prayer she thought of faithful Abraham's trial regarding Isaac, and she felt that God was just as able to carry her through temptation or test, if she submitted all to his will.

Mr. Worthington gave his consent for one of the children to go for a visit. The aunt having chosen Bessie, hasty preparations were made for their departure. As the mother kissed her curly-haired little girl good-by, her heart seemed bursting with sorrow. She tried to control her feelings, but only God knew the wound that her aunt's parting words made. "Use your influence in my behalf, Niece, with your husband, in case we want to keep Bessie," she had said, and then the great train moved slowly from the station. Abraham was all the mother could think of on her return home. Oh! would God give her back her child?

Letter after letter came, each telling how fond the aunt and her husband were of Bessie and how happy she was in her new home, but not a word about her return. Four, five, six weeks passed. Then one day a letter came stating that they had decided not to adopt a child now and that, as Bessie was getting homesick, the parents might expect her home the next day. Then, it had been only a test! Oh, how glad Mrs. Worthington was that she had been faithful. Yes, her God was the very same God that Abraham had served centuries before. It was hard to wait until train-time the next day. When once more the loving mother held her darling child in her arms, the tears that could not flow for weeks streamed freely.

Bessie was glad to be at home again. After the cold, formal, loveless life at her aunt's, she appreciated her own humble home more than ever before.

But a far greater test was waiting the dear mother—one that would call for more than human strength to bear.

After Bessie's return Mrs. Worthington put forth every effort to teach her children more about heavenly things. She bore in mind the scripture, "Train up a child in the way it should go; and when it is old, it will not depart from it." As she did not want to fail along this line, she spent every spare moment with her children. And she seldom let them go from home to visit unaccompanied by her; but one day, being very busy, she let them go alone to their grandmother's. The distance was not great, and Bessie, now nearly six years old, knew the way perfectly. All would have been well had their grandmother been at home. She being away, the girls stopped to watch some children at play. These children were breaking old bottles that they had picked up in the alley. As the little girls stood watching the sport, a large brown bottle was brought forth and with a heavy stroke of the hammer was broken. Small pieces of the glass flew in every direction. One piece struck Louise on the palm of the hand just below the thumb, knocking off the skin, but not producing a wound deep enough to bleed. Her grandmother, who appeared on the scene just at this time, examined the wound. She though it would soon be all right, but bound it up with a cloth to satisfy the child. The children played as usual and then returned home in time for supper.

When they came in, their mother, who had been very busy through the day at housecleaning, was preparing a hasty supper, and she gave them no special attention. The family were soon seated around the supper-table. They had not been there long until Mrs. Worthington noticed that Louise was not eating. She asked the child why she did not eat, but received no reply. On being asked if her throat was sore, Louise nodded her head. Still the mother did not think the child's condition serious; and, after pinning a flannel around the child's neck, she did the evening work and prepared to attend a prayer-meeting. She had noticed the rag upon Louise's hand, but Bessie had laughed about the little cut and said, "Grandma tied it up just to please Louise."

Although the meeting that night was unusually good, Mrs. Worthington could not forget the expression on her child's face as they had kissed each other good-by. It seemed to be before her all the time; so she really felt relieved when the meeting closed and she could return.

Upon entering her home she immediately asked her husband, "How is Louise?" He answered that she had been very naughty and cross and that he had been obliged to punish her. This news increased the mother's fears. Feeling of the child's head, she found it hot and feverish.

As Louise continued to grow worse, at two o'clock in the morning Mrs. Worthington thought it best to examine the child's throat; but when the mother asked the little girl to open her mouth, she said, "Mama, I can't."

"What!" exclaimed the mother, "you can not open your mouth! Why, child, what is the matter with you?" Although Louise tried repeatedly to open her mouth, she could force her teeth apart only about an eighth of an inch, and only with great difficulty could she speak.

By this time Mr. Worthington had fully awakened to the fact that something serious was troubling his child, and he sprang to her side. As soon as possible they summoned a doctor. He found that the cut on her hand had caused lockjaw, but said that there was no cause for alarm. The parents, however, felt very anxious and called in several doctors for consultation. They found that it was too late to do anything for the child. "The course of this disease," said the doctors, "is usually very rapid; and we are sorry that we can offer no hope."

When Mrs. Worthington heard the doctors' verdict, anguish such as she had never experienced before filled her soul. Her thoughts went back to the previous night. Oh! why had she not examined the child closely then? In her distress she cried to the Lord, saying, "Dear Lord, what can this mean? Must I go through another test with one of my children? If so, help me to say amen to thy will!"

Everything possible was done for the comfort of the little sufferer. The little life was swiftly nearing its close. Even when the doctors injected medicine into her arm to relieve her pain, she did not murmur. Forgetful for a moment of her suffering, she looked into her mother's eyes and said, "Mama, I love you"; then turning to her father, "Papa, I love you"; and then to the doctors and friends, "I like all these folks."

What a beautiful testimony? She had only kindly feelings in her heart for all, even for the doctors, who seemed to be her enemies. Her words were as a message sent from God as they fell into that mother's heart. They seemed as sweet incense and a soothing balm to her troubled spirit. Gazing into the child's face, the mother read of the tender, compassionate love of God for suffering humanity; she read of the depth of Christ's love for the innocent and pure; and, by the heavenly smile that lighted the little face as her darling sank into unconsciousness, she saw that the child realized her Savior's presence.

Slowly the tide is going out; the soul of the child is passing from the mother's presence into life immortal. "O my darling, speak to me once more!" The large blue eyes slowly unclose; a look of disappointment comes into them as she says, "Where has Jesus gone?" The dear eyes softly close; she sinks again into unconsciousness; the beautiful expression of happiness returns; the mother knows that her darling is in the arms of Jesus and is content.

Mrs. Worthington did not sorrow as those who have no hope; for she knew that her heavenly Father knew best, and she could look up with confidence and say, "The Lord gave, and the Lord hath taken away: blessed be the name of the Lord." With the father it was different. Up to this time he had never had any serious thoughts of a future life. He knew that his wife was a good woman, but he considered her religious views rather strange. She had seen so much error among the popular religious denominations and had felt such bondage when meeting with them, that she worshiped with a few spiritual people in a little prayer-meeting. Because of this peculiarity, he had even feared that her mind was affected; but now, when he saw her fortitude under deep trial, he felt that surely there was an unseen power supporting her—a power that he secretly longed to possess, although the time for attaining it he set indefinitely in the future.

As Louise had been his idol, his grief was deep. It stirred his whole being. Her last testimony had convinced him that there is a Savior, that he is interested in mankind, and that he is able to keep in every affliction. Standing by the cold, lifeless form of his little daughter, he promised God that he would meet her in heaven.

After these things Mrs. Worthington realized more keenly than ever the value of confidence between children and parents. With renewed energy she sought daily to strengthen that cord which now seemed to her almost divine. Her daily talks now contained a richer and deeper meaning to Bessie, whose understanding of heavenly things was growing clearer since her sister's death. Through her mother's teaching she gained a knowledge of God and spiritual life that would have taken her many, many years to comprehend had she been left to herself.

Mrs. Worthington was surprised and pleased to note Bessie's confidence in her mother's teaching. One day, in answer to the assertion of a little neighbor girl that Louise was not alive, but dead and buried, Bessie said, "I know Sister's body is dead and buried, but her soul is living with Jesus. He was waiting for her when she died and took her soul away with him."

"I am glad, my child," said her mother, sometime after this conversation, "that you love to come to me with things that trouble you; for as you're going to school now, you can not help hearing and seeing many things that I would rather keep from you until you're older. You'll see and hear many things that you should allow no place in your life; but if you'll always come to me, I'll instruct you so that they'll not be harmful to you. When I was a child, how I longed for some one in whom I could confide! My mother was a good woman, but she didn't realize how I often longed to unburden my heart to her. Father understood this desire, and we often had confidential talks.

"I shall never forget my gratitude when he took me upon his knee one day and told me about many dangers young girls must meet and explained how I might avoid them. His words were just in time; for I had often been allowed to spend the evening at the home of a little friend, who, like myself, was not taught how to meet danger. At first our play had been innocent sports, but a short time before my father's talk a cousin had come to board with the family and attend school. He at once encouraged us to play a game of cards with him. As I knew nothing of the evil of card-playing, I was eager to learn; for he gave me much praise and allowed me to win very often, always rewarding me with a pile of candy. The appearance of so much candy in my possession had led to my father's talk. As father unfolded the nature of card-playing and gambling, a horror for them that has never left me came into my heart. After this I often sought my father's counsel; his faithful admonitions and tender words of encouragement caused me to have more and more confidence in him."

Mrs. Worthington sighed deeply as she continued, "The memory of my dear father is sacred, Bessie. Many times I've thanked the Lord that my father knew the worth of prayer and the value of the confidence of his children. He helped me to tide over the most critical period of my life, and I love to recall the encouragement of his devoted life."

CHAPTER VI.

CONSCIENCE.

One day when Bessie was about eight years old, she said: "Mama, you've often told me that if I'd listen to the voice of conscience it would keep me out of danger. What is conscience? I don't understand."

"My dear child," answered her mother, "your happiness depends upon a pure conscience, one that is void of offense. By the Lord's help, I will gladly explain. Conscience is that which causes us to feel bad when we do what we've been taught to be wrong. At first it is very tender and active. Then, no matter how enticing the temptation, the conscience will warn one not to yield. You've heard your conscience speaking to you, haven't you, Bessie?"

"Yes, Mama," answered Bessie; "that was why I wanted to know more about it. I thought at first it was some person speaking; but when I remembered you had told me that we each have a conscience to tell us to do right, I knew it must be the voice of conscience."

"When it speaks, you must listen," said Mrs. Worthington. "Give heed to its warnings. This little story will show you how careful we should be to heed the warning voice of conscience.

"'Wishing to arise at an early hour each morning, a gentleman purchased an alarm-clock. He took it home, and, having set it, went to bed and slept soundly. In the morning, to the gentleman's great delight, the clock aroused him, so that he was able to get to work in time.

"'For a time he would spring out of bed as soon as the alarm sounded, and the clock never failed to wake him. One morning, however, on hearing the clock sound its usual alarm, he awoke, but, feeling a little sleepy, he lay back on his pillow, thinking that he would get up in a short time. In a few minutes he fell asleep, and did not awake again until very late. He dressed hastily, and, missing his breakfast, hurried away to his work. He resolved not to be so foolish again, and for a time did better; but in a few days he had again overslept. He became more and more neglectful, failing time after time to heed the alarm. At length it only partially aroused him, and he soon slumbered again. Day by day it disturbed him less, until at last it did not arouse him at all, although it sounded as loudly as ever.'

"So will it be with your conscience. If you don't heed its voice, you'll hear it speaking less loudly each day until its voice will at last cause you no discomfort. You'll then be in a very dangerous moral condition. No one but

God can help you out. This is one reason why, Bessie, many people can do things that you can not.

"Satan aimed his first blow at the conscience; for if he can silence it, then he can lead the soul deeper and deeper into sin."

CHAPTER VII.

A DOWNWARD STEP.

"I have good news for you, Bessie," said Mrs. Worthington as Bessie came skipping into the room from her play. "Your papa and I have decided to leave our little home here in Chicago and buy a home in Michigan."

"Oh, how nice!" exclaimed Bessie, who was still in her eighth year. "Shall we live with Aunt Emma again?"

"Yes, or rather she will live with us," said her mother, smiling. "Your auntie's health is very poor, and she is tired of the responsibility of farming; so we'll relieve her."

The following weeks were happy ones for Bessie. The Lord had been good to her in many ways. He had given her a little baby brother to love and care for, and now she was about to have a pleasant home in the country. She had not forgotten the good times she had enjoyed on the farm with her little sister, and she was very eager for the month of August to come, the time when the family was to move. At last the time came to start. With beating heart Bessie counted the hours that must pass before she could run in the orchard and eat the luscious fruit.

It was late in the afternoon when the Worthington family arrived at their new home. The greetings over, Bessie was contemplating a ramble where she had noticed some large red apples hanging; but just then her aunt said, "Bessie, you must not pick any of the fruit on the place this summer, as the farm is rented and the fruit does not belong to us." This was such a disappointment to the little girl that she could not restrain her tears.

As the days passed by, she often looked longingly toward the tree where hung the beautiful apples, but she never once thought of pulling one, for her mother had carefully taught her the great evil of stealing. "But oh!" thought Bessie, "if only one of the apples would fall upon the ground, I could pick it up, and I wouldn't be stealing it." With this wish in her heart, she daily watched the trees in hopes that just one would fall.

At last her hope was realized. Walking through the orchard one day after a hard wind-storm, she spied several large red apples lying in the soft sand. With a fast-beating heart, she hastened to pick them all up; and, placing them carefully in her apron, she hurried to the house, oft repeating to herself, "I didn't steal them, for the wind blew them off."

As she entered the house, she began to tell how she came by the apples, but stopped in dismay, for she saw her mother's look of disapproval. Very tenderly Mrs. Worthington took her little daughter aside and, sitting down by her, said: "My dear, you don't understand what you've done: those apples are as truly stolen as if you had picked them from the tree. You must take them to Mrs. S. and explain that you didn't know you were stealing them. Taking little things and trying to ease the conscience by saying, 'It doesn't amount to anything,' causes the conscience to fall asleep and to cease its activity. Thus the evil habit of taking what doesn't belong to us becomes a part of our nature, and step by step we fall into greater sin.

"I once heard of a young man who was about to be hanged upon the gallows. Just before the fatal moment he received permission to speak to any of his friends, if he desired. Calling for his aunt, who had reared him, he moved forward as if to speak to her, but instead he bit off her ear. Amid the exclamations of horror that followed, the young man said: 'You think what I have done is cruel. Let me tell you that, had my aunt done her duty by me, I should not be here today. Had she taken the pains to inquire where I obtained the lead pencils, knives, handkerchiefs, and other small articles which I brought home from time to time; had she not accepted the flimsy excuse that I had found them; had she warned me of my danger, and not praised me for "finding" the things I had stolen,—I might have escaped this awful end.'

"So, Bessie, you can see the danger of allowing anything like this—though it does appear a trifle—to pass by unnoticed. You may go and return the apples to Mrs. S., who is now in the orchard."

The lesson was severe and lasting; and as Bessie returned the apples to their rightful owner, it settled deep into her heart.

Parents, beware. Through neglect, the habit of lying begins. An untruth is passed over carelessly and the child allowed to cover up its sins without realizing their sinfulness. Likewise, many other evil habits that have wrecked lives and brought sorrow and disgrace into homes may be traced to the same carelessness on the part of parents and friends.

CHAPTER VIII.

A WISE DECISION.

The lake in front of the Worthington home, though nearly five miles in length, had too small a harbor to permit the entrance of the large Chicago boats. It was therefore necessary, each evening in summer, for small steamboats to gather up the fruit from the farms along the lake and to carry it to the nearest port for large steamers. It was interesting to see the piles of berry crates loaded upon the steamer from the docks extending out into the lake. At such times a crowd of young people frequently arranged to go for a pleasant ride on Lake Michigan, and a few times Bessie had gone.

There was to be such an excursion on the occasion of which I wish to speak, and the young people expected to attend a circus in a city close to the haven to which they were going. Bessie wished very much to go. She soon obtained her father's consent, but went to her mother with many misgivings, for she knew that her mother never went to a circus and that she had always spoken against her going at other times.

Mrs. Worthington was very busy, but she always had time to advise her daughter and to hear her requests. She listened carefully to every word her daughter had to say, and then remained silent for a few minutes. At length she said: "Bessie, there are many things to consider about your going. You know how I love to have you go for a ride on the water when I know you are in good company. I also love to have you attend places of interest to you, when I know there's nothing to defile your mind or lead you from the path of purity. But, Daughter, there are many things in the world that look beautiful to the eye but tend to lead the soul astray. Do you think Jesus would go to a circus? Do you think you could get any good should you go? You have passed your tenth birthday. I think you're old enough to take this matter to God in prayer and let him decide it for you. Go and ask him to direct you to some passage of Scripture that will open your understanding and help you to know what he wants you to do."

"Oh, mama," said Bessie, who had felt strange about the matter, "please tell me yes or no, and I'll say no more about it."

"No, Bessie; it will, in many ways, be better for you to do as I've said," answered her mother tenderly but decisively.

Very reluctantly Bessie left the room, and, taking her Bible, whispered a prayer that she might open it to something that would help her to decide. As she opened the book, her eyes fell upon these words: "Vanity of vanities, saith the preacher, vanity of vanities; all is vanity." Hurriedly she turned the pages, thinking that she might perhaps have opened to that passage anyway. Next she read, "I said in mine heart, Go to now, I will prove thee with mirth; therefore, enjoy pleasure: and behold this also is vanity." Returning to her mother, she read the words, but ended by saying, "I might have turned to that anyway."

"Bessie," said Mrs. Worthington, "those words were written by the wisest man the world has ever known, one who had the privilege of enjoying every known pleasure under the sun. But when he had tried them all, he sat down and wrote the words you have just read, and also said, 'All is vanity and vexation of spirit.' Now you have my view of the subject, and you have Solomon's; but if you are still in doubt, go and pray."

Bessie was not satisfied. She slipped away the second time and fell upon her knees. She cried, "O Lord, you once answered Gideon with a sign; now please give me a sign and help me to know whether I should stay at home or not. If you don't want me to go, make it rain." Though simple and short, the prayer came from the heart. She was determined to know God's will concerning her; and to such God never turns a deaf ear.

The next morning she went to the door and looked at the sky. The day was perfect. The sun was shining brightly, and a cool, gentle breeze was blowing. Just one tiny cloud was in the sky, and that seemed to be floating toward the sun. As she watched the cloud, she saw it gradually increase in size, and at last down came the rain in great drops. Nothing further was needed to convince Bessie that God wanted her to remain at home; and now her staying was no longer a cross to her.

She ran to her father and explained that God did not want her to go, telling him about her prayer and its answer. Her childish words and simple faith touched her father's proud heart, but all he said was, "It's all right, Bessie; but you'll go down to the landing and say good-by to your friends, won't you?"

As she told the girls why she could not go with them and watched the gay party leave the shore, she was not sad, but happy. She kept thinking how kind the dear Lord had been to answer her prayer so wonderfully. When bedtime came, she rested sweetly, having no wounded conscience to trouble or accuse her.

But how about the excursion party? They had an ideal trip on Lake Michigan, attended the show, and started to return. The breeze that had been so gently blowing through the day began to increase at sunset, and by the late hour of their return it had become a gale. But not realizing the fierceness of the storm, they started home. When they reached their own harbor, they found that they could not enter with safety; so they anchored the boat and spent the remainder of the night on the wildly tossing waves. In the morning the wind gradually died away, and the weary, seasick crowd made their way home.

When Bessie learned of their serious experience, she appreciated more than ever the Lord's goodness in leading her to stay at home.

CHAPTER IX.

SELF-CONTROL.

Mrs. Worthington was greatly encouraged when she saw what a blessing her little girl had received from what appeared to be a sore trial. She felt that the time was opportune to plant the seed of self-control within the young heart. In a little while she found an opportunity to begin.

"Bessie," she began when ready for the talk, "I have some important things to tell you today. I wish to speak of your future. There comes a time in the life of every girl when she must change from childhood to womanhood; she can not always remain a child. Until this time arrives, she is very dependent and must lean entirely upon her parents' advice; but as her mind begins to mature, she should be taught the necessity of weighing matters well and of finding out God's will.

"Until the present time all you have done has been at the suggestion of your parents, but it will be different in the future. With your teaching, you are able to look to God for a part of your direction. I shall continue to advise, and, if necessary, to punish you; but I want you to take things to the Lord in prayer and become satisfied within your heart that my advice is according to the Word of God. You must not think you haven't needed the teaching and the guidance you've had thus far in life; and you'll need more careful training than you've ever had. The point I want to impress upon your mind is that there's an element within you, called self, that you must learn to control. At times self will arise and cause you to feel that you know some things even better than Mama. That is the time to remember that Mama has had more experience than you; that her judgment is better than yours; and that you must rely upon it until God helps you to see a matter as she sees it. That was the way you gained the blessing from that experience a few days ago. In this way you will learn the lessons that are so important to your future.

"There are many other things, my dear, that I want to talk to you about soon, but you must be patient a little longer. In the meantime, however, you may ask me any question you please, and I'll answer you. Don't go to other girls with these things, but come to me. I'm always glad to explain to you anything that seems strange. When you're old enough to desire the knowledge and to form the questions, you're old enough to receive an answer to your questions. Come to me often: what seems strange to both of us we can take to God in prayer, and let him teach us.

"Another thing you must do is to turn away from bad associates. Avoid girls who say, 'I'll tell you something if you'll promise not to tell your mother.'

Remember that anything you could not tell me would not be worth hearing; for it's sure to be something unclean or vulgar. Conversing with such girls won't help you to draw close to the Lord nor to know his will concerning you. Much less would it help you to meditate upon the pure and holy things of God. To elevate your soul, Bessie, you must become serious, and seek only those companions whose conversation is kind, gentle, and modest. I believe your desire is to become more like Jesus and to prepare for heaven. So, my child, meditate upon God, and you will grow in the grace and knowledge of Christ. Misspent moments are so much of life and character thrown away; be careful to use them all in God's service.

"Here's a little poem you may learn. It may help you to control self and to value your moments as you should."

MY MOMENTS.

Oh, my precious little moments,
Gliding now so swiftly by;
May I each one spend for Jesus
Ere I see them past me fly.

May I lade each one with something
To be borne to God above,
Fill each full of deeds worth counting,
That will prove my perfect love.

For I would not have them enter
Through those portals bright and fair
Bearing not a single token
For my Master waiting there.

Golden moments, as you carry
Trophies on your upward flight,
Take my character to Jesus;
For I've kept it clean and white.

CHAPTER X.

PARENTAL CONTROL.

Mrs. Worthington was not only a prayerful mother, but a mother wise in home government. Her wisdom, however, came from God. Many a time she felt incapable of giving the advice her young daughter needed; but she always remembered the scripture which reads, "If any of you lack wisdom, let him ask of God, that giveth to all men liberally, and upbraideth not; and it shall be given." After she had spent a season in prayerful meditation, God would supply the words and understanding. Thus she could say with the apostle Paul, that her strength was made perfect in weakness, because her dependence was in Christ.

O mothers, let us learn that God, the Author of home and families, is always interested in the quality and the training of the children. He does not create to cast aside. Neither does anything come by chance. He wills that each tender human plant be nourished and cherished until well fitted to fill its place and calling in life. In childhood's dependent days, the parents should be all to the children that they can not be to themselves. It is not enough that your child be well fed and clothed; its young mind must be guided into proper channels. What work is more noble, more elevating than the teaching of the undeveloped mind? Let not the duties of life nor the claims of society so press upon you as to cause you to neglect your child's character or its education in either temporal or spiritual matters.

As Solomon says, "Take away the little foxes that destroy the vines." It is the little things passed carelessly by that grow larger and larger, and stronger and stronger, within the young heart until at last the unsuspecting parents awake in alarm to behold their child in dreadful bondage. Beware! Guard your child every moment it is under your care. You can not go as companion to your child upon the street or to school, but your influence may attend his every path through life. Do not be discouraged should you hear him use a slang word, but take him at once and tenderly tell him what slang phrases will lead to. Do not speak harshly, but explain in the most loving manner possible. In this way you will cultivate in him a distaste for impure language. A pure, refined nature will be the result. Moreover, as that child realizes through your faithful instruction, the true meaning of sin, he will make you his confidant and will come to you rather than seek the counsel of younger companions. Thus you will be able to control his mind and to instil within his mind pure and upright desires.

Within your home is the place to shine for God. There is no greater field of labor. A Christian mother's influence among the young can not be too highly valued. No one can fill your place in the hearts of your children. Another can provide their temporal needs, but nobody can take the place of Mother. No one else can enter into the daily trials as you can. Nothing else can soothe the wounded feelings as well as a tender embrace or a word from mother. Be liberal, dear mothers, with these tokens of sympathy, so sweet to your child; and think not for one moment that you are not fulfilling God's plan concerning you or that moments thus spent are wasted. It is only a short time at best that we can be blessed with the privilege of instructing our children.

CHAPTER XI.

CHRISTIAN EXPERIENCE.

As Bessie grew older, Mrs. Worthington chose the twilight hour for confidential talks with her daughter. Both looked forward to these times with pleasure. Each evening after the daily duties were ended, Bessie might be found sitting at her mother's feet. Here she related the many happenings of the day and in turn received instruction and advice from the one who held her confidence. Here the mother taught her child the secret of true devotion. She instructed Bessie that prayer, good reading, and meditation are the keys to use to unlock God's great storehouse of blessings. She pointed to the Bible as a pattern by which to fashion one's life, pointing out to her the many scriptures bearing upon different subjects and telling her how every modest, earnest Christian ought to dress and act in order to adorn the gospel of Christ. She encircled the word "purity" with such a halo of glory that she awakened within the heart of her child a determination ever to live so pure a life that she would not only keep herself stainless but also help others to that sacred and elevated plane.

Upon one of these occasions, when Bessie was in her twelfth year, she said: "Mama, why don't we go to the meetings that are being held at the schoolhouse on Sunday? The girls have asked me several times, and I have told them I didn't know. They have a minister from a distance, and he has taken the names of all who want to join the church."

"That is a deep subject, my child," said Mrs. Worthington. "I have often wished to explain to you my reasons for not attending the public services held in our neighborhood by the different denominations, but have feared you were still too young to understand, for the matter seems hard even for some older persons to comprehend. But I will tell you and trust the Lord to make it plain.

"My parents taught me that it was my duty to attend religious services at least once a week. This I did, and professed to be a Christian until I was a young woman. I knew that I loved the Lord and wanted to do right, but found that I could not always do right in my own strength. I was daily doing things that displeased the Lord. I became so troubled about my condition that one day I went to the minister, and, telling him how I felt, requested him to pray for me and to help me to get a real Bible experience. In answer to my request, he only smiled and said, 'You are too particular. You might as well try to split a hair as to try to live a holy life in this world.'

"As I returned home that day, I was very sad indeed. Oh, how much I longed to be like Jesus, whom God had given me as an example! I knew the Bible taught that if we expect to enter heaven we must live a pure and holy life. I was determined to do this—but how was I to do it? To whom could I go for help? Most of the church-members were so worldly-minded they thought of little else than a good time, and the few spiritual ones were afraid to tell how they felt, for fear of their minister's displeasure.

"At last I decided to seek from God and his Word what my soul was longing for. As I sought, I began to see I had been deceived. I found that as God looked upon mankind, he could see only two classes of people—the righteous and sinners; and I saw that I was a sinner.

"By reading the twelfth chapter of First Corinthians, I learned that Christ's body is the church; that to become a member of the church my name must be written in heaven; that every Christian in the world is my brother or sister in Christ; the Lamb's book of life is the only class-book in which our names need to be recorded; and that our names are removed only because of our turning again to sin. To me these thoughts were both new and marvelous. I saw that every saved person in the different denominations is a Christian and a member of God's true church, but I knew that such persons were unable to worship God aright for fear of displeasing their ministers or of breaking some of the church-rules. And when I read in 2 Cor. 6:14 that we are not to be unequally yoked together with unbelievers, I felt that I must come out and stand alone. This I promised God to do at any cost, and asked him to give me a Bible experience. He answered my prayer; and I was so happy that I walked the floor for a long time, clapping my hands and praising God.

"Because of the course I had taken many misunderstood me and thought I was partially insane. Even your dear papa thinks so still, but I dare not grieve God by going back.

"I have had some dreams that have greatly encouraged me. The first was given while I was wondering why I could not find any one who believed the whole Bible. I seemed to be standing in a meeting-house; the service was ended and nearly every one had gone home. I noticed a woman in great distress. Going to her, I found that she had a very sore hand and that she was alone, with no one to help her home through the darkness. With her consent, I quickly picked her up in my arms and carried her safely through a long, dark, narrow passage. As we passed along, I spoke words of encouragement to her. Suddenly we came out into a large open field carpeted with flowers, and there I laid her down, saying, 'How nicely we have gotten along alone.' Then I awoke.

"For some time I could not see the meaning of the dream. At last I understood that the afflicted woman was I myself and that the Savior wanted to carry me through the dark and dangerous way of life alone.

"At another time I dreamed I was riding on a locomotive. Again I was alone. The seat that I was sitting on was so small I had to be very careful lest I be injured by the machinery around me. I didn't think of danger while the train was in motion; but as it drew up at a certain station, I began to consider my position. The thought came, 'What will people think of me? They will certainly say I am stealing a ride.' I remembered my ticket, and, placing my hand upon it, I felt satisfied. At the next station I could see inside of the passenger coaches. I had a good view of the passengers in one of the coaches, and I recognized the prominent members of the denomination I had lately left. As they sat in their cushioned seats, carelessly talking to one another, they all seemed happy and contented. My own condition then arose before me, and I felt lonely indeed and thought, 'I will step down from my little seat and enter the coach with the rest.' I was just about to do this—even had my hand upon the door knob—when I realized that I had left my dress in the little seat, and again I awoke.

"The dream seemed very plain in every way. My ticket was my experience and title to heaven, and the dress left up in the tiny seat was the robe of Christ's righteousness. While alone and contented, I was all right, but to return to the denomination would mean to leave both robe and title behind.

"Still, God has given me some devoted Christian friends, who are willing to live as the Bible directs, and with these I worship as you know, dear, in our little weekly prayer-meetings. I trust that some day your father will see and will understand me better, and that we can worship God together. But I will be faithful even though I should be forced to walk alone.

"Now, dear, I trust you can see that the true church is Christ's body and that every soul is a member as long as he continues to live a pure and holy life. Whether he is a member of some sect or not, sin will cut him off; and if he continues to profess as I did, he is a hypocrite in God's sight. 'Come out from among them and be ye separate' is a command that every Christian should obey."

CHAPTER XII.

THE BEAUTIFUL SECRET.

The mother's talks about her own Christian experience enabled Bessie to understand the beautiful secret of salvation—an influence that was to beautify her character and to mold her whole subsequent career. Bessie's developing mind was able to grasp firmly the golden thread of religious truth, which, unraveling from the tangle of sectism, had guided her faithful mother into the fulness of divine truth.

Thus it was—

In the gentle hush of evening,
When the sun sank in the west;
When the little bird was nestling
In its quiet, sheltered nest;
When the stars were brightly shining
From the lofty sky above,
Bessie learned the lovely secret
Of her Savior's perfect love.

In the twilight's deep'ning shadows,
At her loving mother's feet,
Sat she often on a hassock,
Hearing words of counsel sweet.
Sacred season was this hour
To the twain in waiting there,
Each the burden of the other
Sought to know and ofttimes share.

As the loving mother listened
To the record of the day,
To the questions of her daughter—

Spoken oft in childish way,
She in tenderness instructed
With the wisdom of the Lord,
Gained by prayer and careful study
Of his precious, holy Word.

There the character was strengthened;
Bessie's heart was made to feel
Greater love for her Creator,
For his work a deeper zeal.
And she saw God's plan for pardon,
To the feet of Jesus came,
And was able, like her mother,
Full salvation then to claim.

Ah! fond mother, learn the secret
That will win thy children dear;
Draw them gently to thy bosom,
Ever seek their hearts to cheer.
From thy home exclude all worry,
Fretful cares, and sad'ning gloom;
But God's sunshine bid a welcome,
Let it shine in ev'ry room.

As a spring within a desert,
Thou mayst water each plant small;
But the plant itself must blossom—
Thou canst tend it, that is all.
Tiny human plants will flourish
In an atmosphere like this,
And will yield good, fruitful blossoms

That will bring true happiness.

Children always thirst for knowledge,
And ere long 'tis surely gained;
If not from a faithful mother,
'Tis from evil source obtained.
Blameless never is the mother
Who will not the trouble take
To instruct her precious children,
Close companions of them make.

Like a florist wise and zealous,
Guard thou well each blossom fair,
Lest the perfume and the sweetness
Vanish for the lack of care.
Choose thou then some place at even
When the daily toils are done,
Where life's many cares and blessings
May be numbered one by one.

God will give thee wisdom, mother,
To supply thine ev'ry need,
As thou givest wholesome knowledge,
When the childish voices plead.
Their young minds, so pure, unfolding,
Will reveal the secret fair
That will prove how great the value
Of a mother's love and pray'r.

CHAPTER XIII.

BLESSING AND TRIAL.

Now that Bessie had learned the secret of a Christian life, she longed to see others enjoying the love of God. She felt the greatest burden for her father. Oh, if she could see him enjoying salvation! She often poured out her desire in prayer, with childlike trust and confidence. God heard her prayers.

One morning as she was passing the barn on her way to school, she heard some strange sounds. Peering through a window, she beheld a sight that made her wonder if she saw aright. There stood her beloved father, great tears streaming from his eyes, his countenance beaming with heavenly peace and joy, and praises to God pouring from his lips. What did it mean? In a weak voice she said, "Papa dear, what is the matter!"

Turning he exclaimed: "Oh, Bessie, God has saved me! I am so happy! Run quick and tell your mother!" Bessie ran to the house to tell the glad news, but her father was there nearly as soon, saying, "Oh, I'm saved! You're right, wife. I know now that you're right, and I see things just as you do! I'm so happy and feel so different. Oh, help me to praise the dear Lord."

Let us leave them in their happiness and follow Bessie to school. Her father's words rang as sweet music in her ears. How good the dear Lord was to answer her in her father's behalf! She felt that no good thing would be withheld from them that walk uprightly. But Bessie was soon to meet a severe and unexpected trial.

Her mother had made her a school-dress. Though neat and pretty, it was of a material commonly used for men's shirts. Bessie knew this, but thought nothing of it until some of her schoolmates gathered round her at recess and said, "O girls, Bessie has a new dress like her father's shirt." Another said, "Perhaps it is his shirt." The remarks were certainly unkind, and Bessie felt them keenly; but she laughed and said, "Yes; I know it." Nothing more was said. But oh, that dress! How she disliked to wear it! At times she could hardly start to school with it on; but then she would think, "I know Mama thought it was pretty when she got it for me; and I thought it was nice until the girls made those remarks. I will try to like it for Mama's sake."

With such thoughts in her mind she returned home from school one evening. When she reached the house, she saw that no one was at home; but, knowing where the key was kept, she easily gained admittance. Finding herself alone in the house, she thought: "Now is the time to learn to like my dress, and I'm going to do it. Mother shall not know how I have felt about it." She hastened into the parlor and stood before a large mirror.

Now, Bessie knew that she did not have a pretty face, and she had gained the victory over that; but she did want to feel that her clothes looked well on her, and that was the battle she meant to fight that evening. As she slowly turned from side to side viewing herself intently, she liked the dress better and better. At last she thought it very pretty and becoming, and she knelt down and thanked God for giving it to her. As she changed it for her work-dress, she wondered why she had allowed the children's remarks to affect her so much and had not appreciated the dress more. No more remarks were ever made about the dress, and Bessie continued to admire it until it was worn out. No one but herself and the Lord knew of the struggle through which she passed.

Through the trial concerning the dress, Bessie learned several valuable lessons: first, the less notice one takes of unkindness, the better; second, God's grace can keep in time of temptation; third, one should not murmur because of persecution; and, last, and best of all, God usually gives his children some great blessing before a severe trial, and the close relationship between the two makes them almost one in effect. She could now say with real appreciation:

A little trial often tries,

But proves a blessing in disguise.

Just as the rough rock holds the gem,

The trial holds my diadem.

But a still greater trial was awaiting her. Bessie had a thirst for knowledge. She was doing well in school and wanted to do better. Instead of taking exercise during the daily intermissions, she often spent them in hard study. Her system, naturally frail, could not stand the strain. She contracted a fever and for three months despaired of life. In the third month dropsy of the chest set in; and, on account of smothering spells, she had to be bolstered up in bed with pillows.

One day as Mrs. Worthington stood beside her child she felt that God wanted to heal her. Kneeling beside the bed, she prayed, "Dear Lord, heal my child, and grant that she may be spared to work for thee." From that time Bessie began to improve. She had no more smothering spells, and before long she was well and strong.

Bessie found a blessing even in this trial. She saw that, had she been able to push ahead as she had desired, she might have lost sight of Jesus, and she now understood that her Savior cared for her body as well as for her soul.

CHAPTER XIV.

THE SURPRISE PARTY.

As soon as Bessie was strong enough to go out, she was invited to stay all night with a friend. She supposed she was to be the only guest, but found that a surprise had been planned for her. A goodly number of her friends and schoolmates were present.

The young folks spent a few hours very pleasantly in playing games, and Bessie enjoyed that part of the evening very much. But late in the evening some one proposed dancing, and the boys began to choose their partners. A very strange feeling came over Bessie when some one asked her to dance. She shook her head and said, "No; I do not know how to dance." Several urged her to try, but she said, "No; I would rather not."

She was the only one that did not dance. As she sat watching the others, she wondered if it were right for boys and girls to act as these were acting. She had never heard that it is wrong to dance, but it did not look or seem right to her. She decided that on reaching home she would ask her mother.

When Bessie got home the next morning, her mother asked, "Well, dear, did you have a good time?"

"Oh, yes," answered Bessie; "most of the time I did." Then she told about the surprise party and about all that had happened, and concluded by asking, "Mama, is it right to dance?"

"I have been thinking for a long time, Bessie, that I ought to have a talk with you about dancing and tell you of some of the evils to which it leads," answered her mother. "Dancing is an amusement that many girls consider very attractive. When asked why they think so, they hardly know what to answer, but generally speak of the music and the graceful motions."

"Oh, Mama, the motions they made at the party last night were anything but graceful. I know you wouldn't have allowed me to do as they did, and I don't want to. It wasn't modest. I never want to go to a dance again."

"I'm so glad, Bessie, you feel as you do about dancing; but, dear, to those who learn, there is something very fascinating about it. Some girls have said they would rather dance than eat; and, with a great many, I believe it is true.

"Men of low character and of evil inclinations regard the dance-hall as a favorable place to betray unsuspecting girls and frequent it for that very purpose. Their victims are usually the sweetest and most trusting girls. Their beauty attracts undesirable attention, and their ignorance makes them an easy prey. O Bessie, there are so many unprincipled men in the world who love to win and betray the confidence of young innocent girls.

"Philosophers tell us that 'perfect happiness comes only from a pleasure attractive to our moral nature in its purity and perfection. If we delight in pleasures of the other sort, our moral natures are degraded.'

"You have noticed the immodest positions taken by those who dance, and you feel a deep sense of shame for them. Should you try to partake of their pleasure, your moral nature would be degraded, and you would in time lose that sense of shame and be as eager for the pleasure as any of the others. Thus yielding, one step at a time, you would cease to look upon the dance as immodest and would find real enjoyment in it, and perhaps would be led into greater sin. It is in this way that many girls lose their virtue. Then they are shunned by their old associates, who are really but a step higher in morality. Forsaken by friends, hopeless as to their future, deserted even by those who wrought their downfall, these poor girls sink lower and lower, and lead lives of shame and misery.

"No spiritual-minded person will take part in worldly amusements, for he can not enjoy them. Christians who indulge in dancing turn away from God and seek fellowship with the world. Such are sure to lose the grace of God from their hearts."

CHAPTER XV.

LEROY'S HEALING.

Bessie's little brother, Leroy, now past five years of age, was far from being rugged. Though he had a full, round face and a large head, his body was emaciated and did not develop properly. He could go only a few steps without falling. He had fainting spells, which gradually increased in frequency and duration.

Many times as Mrs. Worthington looked at her poor little boy, she lifted her heart to God in earnest prayer to know his will concerning the child. Many friends remarked that she would never be able to bring him up; but she knew that, if for the best, God could heal the child and give him right development.

At last his illness became very serious. One night his head was burning with fever, while his body was cold and clammy. It seemed but a question of time until he would pass away.

As Mrs. Worthington looked at her child, she remembered the words, "Man's extremity is God's opportunity," and "The prayer of faith shall save the sick." She wondered why God had brought them to her mind. She began to ask herself: "Do I believe that God can heal that child? If it is God's will to take him, can I submit?" To the first question she answered, "Yes; God made him," and to the second, "Thy will be done, O God." Then she breathed an earnest prayer for his healing. The sweet assurance came that her prayer was answered; that the child would grow well and strong. She felt that she could lie down by his side and trust him in the hands of the One who gave him.

She placed a wet cloth on his head, lay down by his side, and knew no more until the next morning. Both slept soundly. When she awoke, she saw that the child was breathing naturally and that the fever was entirely gone. Then she fully realized that God had healed him. With a grateful heart she thanked the Lord for his tender love. It was indeed true that Leroy was well. About ten o'clock his mother carried him to the lake and, having Bessie to row the boat, gave him a pleasant boat-ride. The fever never returned; his head stopped growing; and he became a strong, healthy boy. The friends who had thought that he would surely die said they could not understand the change that had taken place, but Mrs. Worthington understood, and gave God all the praise.

CHAPTER XVI.

EXPLAINING THE DIVINE LIFE.

After Bessie's conversion Mrs. Worthington's talks to her were often on the subject of the divine life within—how to care for it and nourish it, so that it might not die nor become blighted. She sometimes compared the young Christian's experience to that of a new-born babe. "You know," said she, "the little one must be carefully fed, and tenderly guarded against everything harmful. Even a slight breeze blowing upon its little body, if unprotected, might result in death. But as the child grows older and stronger, it gradually becomes accustomed to the rude elements about it and can, with comparative safety, be brought in contact with them. The Christ life, new-born in the human heart, is just as sensitive and needs the same tender care. Guard it carefully, Bessie. It must be constantly nourished by prayer and the Word of God. Seek to become established by the grace of sanctification; then you will be better able to meet temptation and persecution. Christ is your shepherd, and he wants to lead you, his lamb, into green pastures and beside still waters.

"A person may profess to be a Christian, Bessie; but unless he has a change of heart and affections, he is what the Bible terms a wolf in sheep's clothing, and not one of the gentle lambs of the Savior's fold. The profession does not amount to anything when the heart is full of envy, hatred, jealousy, love of self, and a drawing toward the world. A person with a profession only, may appear for a time to be quite lamb-like; but sooner or later the old nature will manifest itself, for it can not be hidden long."

"I think, Mama," said Bessie, "I understand you—but you spoke of the experience of sanctification; please tell me what that means."

As briefly as possible, the mother explained that the second cleansing of the heart takes away that evil nature which causes man to want to disobey God.

Not long after this talk Bessie had an experience in school that helped her to comprehend her mother's words. To be put back in her studies was hard, but to have to give up her old teacher, to whom she was strongly attached, was harder still. Her regret on the latter account, however, was of short duration; for her new teacher was even more lovable than the old one, and, best of all, she was a Christian. She and Bessie not only got along well, but became warm friends and enjoyed sweet fellowship in the Spirit. One day, however, something happened that severely tested their love, but, in the end, only deepened it.

Bessie's seatmate, a girl named Nora, about Bessie's own age, was very mischievous. She did so many things deserving punishment that the teacher was often perplexed to know what course to take with her. Some one has said that "misery likes company." This was certainly true of Nora. She knew that the teacher and Bessie were good friends, and she longed to see Bessie get into trouble and receive some punishment. Knowing that Bessie tried hard to obey the rules of the school, Nora saw that she should have to lay some cunning plan or she should not realize her wish. She began to watch for an opportunity.

A streamlet ran past the schoolhouse. While Bessie and Nora were playing near it one day, Bessie fell down in some mud. Just as she fell, the school-bell rang and they had to hurry back to their lessons. Fearing that some of the mud might have splattered on her face, Bessie asked if her face was clean. Nora answered quickly, "Oh yes; do hurry up." Nora felt that her chance had come, and she made up her mind to get her seatmate into trouble, if possible. Hurrying into the schoolroom, she whispered to one of the boys, telling him to ask Bessie as she passed what was the matter with her face, but to say nothing more. When Bessie came down the aisle, she saw this boy looking at her with an amused expression, and gave him close attention. As she passed him, he whispered, "Bessie, what is the matter with your face?" and then turned quickly away. Fully convinced that her face was dirty, Bessie sat down very much ashamed. Nora knew how her seatmate would feel and prepared herself for the question that she was sure would be asked. As it was time for the writing-lesson, she stuck her finger in inks of different colors; and, when Bessie asked where her face was dirty, she quickly pointed out the places, each time leaving a large spot of ink. Bessie, wholly unconscious of the ink-spots on her face, thought what a dreadful sight she must be, and asked permission of the teacher to wash. When the teacher turned, she saw, not mud, but ugly ink-spots. Supposing that Bessie had put them there, she shook her head. Her surprise was great. She felt that she ought to do something about it; but, being undecided, she turned away.

Bessie became much worried; for many eyes were turned upon her, and some of the pupils were laughing. She wanted to hide, but could not, and kept wondering why a little mud should cause so much amusement. One girl, Anna, tried secretly to pass her a wet handkerchief, but this Nora quickly caught from her and hid. Poor Bessie was now ready to cry, and again asked permission to wash her face; but her teacher answered, "No; you must go to writing."

Bessie naturally had a high temper and was inclined to be stubborn when she felt that she was being imposed upon; but she had always held her temper in subjection, as she knew it to be wrong to give way to anger. On this occasion, however, it seemed impossible to control herself. When the teacher said, "Go to writing," Bessie obeyed; but she was so angry that she hardly knew what she was doing. Suddenly she thought, "If I daub a lot of ink on my face, perhaps she will let me wash"; and she rubbed some on with her finger. But alas! this did not work as she had expected. The teacher saw her put it on and concluded that she had put the other on also; so she said, "Bessie, you may go and sit in my chair." As she said this, all the stubbornness in Bessie's nature arose. She did not move; and when the teacher said sternly, "Are you going to obey?" she shook her head and caught hold of the seat. At this moment Nora whispered, "If that were me, she'd make me go." The teacher heard the words and looked first at Nora and then at Bessie. She hesitated for a moment, then walked over to Bessie, took her by the shoulders and jerked her from the seat, and then dragged her up to the chair and set her down, telling her to study. "I have no book," retorted Bessie. The teacher ordered one brought, and, leaving her, went to her other duties.

What a moment for Bessie! Too angry to study, she sat there thinking of the dreadful scene she had created. Her heart burned with shame. Oh! what could she do?

Anna, the girl who had tried to hand her the wet handkerchief, had noticed all of Nora's actions and had determined to help Bessie, if possible. On pretext of looking up a word in the dictionary, Anna went forward, laid a wet rag where Bessie could reach it, and returned to her seat. Bessie eagerly took the rag and rubbed her face. She was surprised to see the different colors of ink appear upon it. How they came to be there she did not know; but she did not think about them long, for something far worse began to trouble her. She knew that she had lost the grace of God out of her heart. Oh, how wretched she felt! Would God forgive her again? Yes; she knew he would; for she had read that, "The Lord is nigh unto them that are of a broken heart, and saveth such as be of a contrite spirit." This thought was a great comfort to her. But, oh! what about her teacher? How could her teacher ever love and respect her again? She would ask her pardon as soon as possible, but would she forgive her?

It was not long until the teacher went to her desk for something, but she took no notice of Bessie. Beaching out very timidly, Bessie touched her and said, "O Miss Harrington, won't you please forgive me?" But the teacher pretended not to hear her, and turned quickly away. The next thought was, "What will Mama think and say? Oh, if only she did not have to know about it!" With these thoughts coursing through her mind, Bessie was unable to study; and by the time school closed, she was in great distress.

After closing the school, the teacher paid no attention to Bessie for some time; but when she had finished her evening duties and all the pupils except Nora, Anna, and Bessie had left the building, she turned to Bessie, fell upon her knees, and threw both arms around her. Bessie sobbed, "Oh, please forgive me! please forgive me!" For some time the teacher made no reply, and Nora muttered, "Catch me asking her forgiveness!" At last the teacher, looking up through tearful eyes, said, "Bessie dear, it is you who must forgive me. I should have been a better example to you this afternoon. Let us pray." Then two sad hearts were lifted to God in humble, earnest prayer that he would forgive them for Jesus' sake. God heard their prayers, gave back the sweet peace that they had lost out of their souls, and bound their hearts together in Christian love and fellowship.

Nora went her way, provoked with her seatmate and angry because the joke had not worked quite as she had expected. Anna, slipping her arm through Bessie's walked home with her and told her all that Nora had done. Bessie was surprised. She understood why things had taken the course they had; but, knowing it was really Satan, who had been trying to overthrow her own soul, she did not censure her seatmate.

Her only thought now was of how sad her mother would feel. Bessie decided that the occurrence was too dreadful to tell her about and that she would keep it a secret. This was her decision until she saw her mother coming down the walk to meet her. Having always told her mother everything, Bessie did not know how it would seem to keep a secret from her; so when they met, she forgot all about her decision and began at once to tell her mother all that had happened.

Mrs. Worthington listened very carefully to Bessie's story and then said: "Bessie, I am so glad you have told me all this yourself, and have held nothing back nor blamed Nora. God will take care of the matter, and I believe that your lesson is a lasting one. And now, my child; you can see your great need of sanctification. Had that ugliness and stubbornness been taken out of your heart, you would have been spared much suffering. I trust that you will earnestly seek and obtain this grace."

It was well that Bessie told her mother everything, for Nora did all in her power to circulate the story and to make it as bad as possible. Nora's mother, thinking it best to tell Mrs. Worthington about Bessie's misbehavior, made a special call at the Worthington home for that purpose. Bessie's mother listened to what her neighbor's story was and then smilingly replied, "Yes, I know all about it; Bessie told me before she reached home. I am so glad that I have the confidence of my child. We are companions; I love her company, and she loves mine." These words sounded strange to the visitor. She could not understand. "It seems strange," said she, "that Bessie loves to stay at home and to be with you so much. Doesn't she ever get lonesome? Nora is restless and tired when she has to stay at home, and says I am too old for her."

Ah! here was the secret of the difference between the two girls. One mother had allowed her daughter to choose her own company and had not inquired into their plays and talks; whereas the other knew the secrets of her child's heart and could advise and instruct her in any matter. Between Bessie and her mother there was a tie of which Nora and her mother knew nothing. "Train up a child in the way he should go: and when he is old he will not depart from it." Prov. 22:6.

CHAPTER XVII.

TEMPTATIONS.

At Christmas time Bessie received the following letter from one of her friends:

> Dear Bessie:
>
> I have long wondered what to send you as a Christmas gift, and it seemed a hard problem to solve. I fear you will wonder at what I am sending; but, knowing that you are nearly thirteen years old and must be growing very fast, I have decided to send you a corset. I hope you will like and appreciate it enough to wear it.
>
> Lovingly your friend,
>
> Lizzie.

On receiving the package, Bessie looked at the corset and said, "Mama, shall I wear it?"

Mrs. Worthington looked anxiously at her daughter; for she knew that Bessie would have strong temptations along this line, as she did not have a pretty form, and was growing rapidly. She had hoped, however, that the subject would not be mentioned for some time. Silently she breathed a little prayer for wisdom to answer the question, and then said:

"Bessie, God used great wisdom in forming your body. He knew just what shape it would have to be in order to perform its natural functions. Do you think it would be proper to try to change it? Do you wonder why something snug around your waist could be harmful? Listen, dear, and I will tell you. Let us take the corset and examine it. It certainly looks very innocent and pretty, but just see how stiff it is. These steel ribs and this whalebone make it more like a piece of harness than anything else I can think of. When worn about the waist, it produces pressure upon the vital organs and thus deforms the body. These long strings at the back are often drawn so tightly as to cause the misplacement and derangement of those organs whose functions are most necessary to health and happiness. As a consequence, many a woman has to suffer long years of torture.

"Many women say they don't wear the corset tight, and think, therefore, that no harm results; but, let one of them put a snug-fitting bandage on any other part of the body, and she will see how quickly the muscles of that part will weaken and decrease in size. Should a young woman who has never worn a corset attempt to wear one about her waist as loosely as they are ever worn, she would, if honest with herself, cast it aside as an abominable thing.

"The reason why Lizzie wants you to begin wearing a corset while you're young is that, if you'll bind your waist before you've reached your full growth, your waist will never attain the size it would have attained under natural conditions. In other words, you would be deformed."

"I don't think I shall ever wear it, Mama, if that's the effect it has upon the body. If God takes such particular care of us that he numbers our very hairs, he must be very much grieved to see any one put a corset about her waist."

"I'm glad for your decision, my child, but you'll soon meet greater temptations. Some mothers don't think it worth while to warn their girls of the dangers that threaten them in regard to love and marriage; but I want to see you, Bessie, fully prepared, so that you may safely pass this dangerous period.

"Most girls at your age have some strange idea regarding love. In the schoolroom, perhaps, a girl notices some particular boy who has a winning way. At first she simply thinks he is nice; is glad to see him promoted, receive honor, etc. Gradually her mind becomes filled with queries concerning his opinion of her. She dares not own that she loves to appear well in his eyes, but it is true nevertheless. During his absence she misses him, and upon his return her heart beats with emotion. If he pays her little attentions, she dwells upon them until she becomes eager for them. Her playmates notice a change in her, for she can no longer hide her feelings. She blushes when mention is made of her preference for him. The couple seek to be together as much as possible, and are soon meeting together secretly. When reproved, they may promise not to let the thing happen again, only to repeat it in a short time. The secrecy of these meetings make them more enjoyable, and their length and frequency are unconsciously increased.

"Satan, who is never asleep upon such occasions, makes reproof his companion to push them forward. Friendly warnings are unheeded; and if force be used to prevent the meetings, the couple may think of eloping. They may not have thought of marriage until this time; but when the girl realizes what she has done, she consents to the hasty marriage. Such marriages, Bessie, seldom result happily.

"The place to stop was at the beginning. She should have gained control of her wandering affections. Young girls who lavish their love upon boys of their own age or older lose relish for other things, and their minds become dwarfed and weakened by being taxed with thoughts that are not fit for them to consider at so early an age.

"It is all right to form in your mind an ideal for your affections, if you don't have in mind some particular person; but your common sense should be your guide. Two rowboats passing each other upon the water are all right as long as they are far enough apart; but let these boats drift or be guided too close together, and there is great danger of a collision. Your affections are to you what the rudder is to the boat, and reason is your pilot. They will guide you aright if you will let them."

"Mama," said Bessie, "there's a girl in our school, only a few months older than I, that says she is to be married in a short time. The man she's to marry is nearly twice as old as she is, too. We told her that she ought to wait until she wore long dresses before she talked about getting married. Don't you think that is dreadful?"

"Yes, dear, it is. No girl should ever be married while she is so young."

CHAPTER XVIII.

ANSWERS TO PRAYER.

During the summer Bessie's cousin John and a boy friend came to visit her. They spent many pleasant hours on the lake. One day while they were about two miles from home, a fierce storm arose. They noticed the sky growing dark and tried very hard to reach home; but, when still some distance from the shore, they could see that instead of making any headway they were drifting before the wind.

It was a serious moment. As the great waves dashed up over them, each adding to the amount of water in the boat, Bessie looked first at her cousin toiling away at the oars, the great drops of perspiration coursing down his face, then at their friend nearly wild with terror, and then at the western sky. "John," said she to her cousin, "I believe that's rain coming toward us." Until then the boy, who was a little older than Bessie, had been brave; but as he turned to look, his face blanched with terror, and he said, "Bessie, if that is rain, it will certainly sink our boat; for, see, it is nearly half full of water now."

The situation was certainly critical, but Bessie felt that it was not the time to despair. She remembered that in olden times Jesus had calmed the sea. Believing that he could still do the same, she prayed for help from heaven. Then, encouraging her cousin to do his best, she, assisted by their friend, began to bale out the water as rapidly as they could. In a few moments the great drops of rain were dashing down upon them. Without speaking, all kept at their work for what seemed to them an hour, but which was really but a short time. Suddenly it ceased raining; and, looking about them, they saw that the lake was perfectly quiet—not a ripple could be seen. With trembling voice Bessie said, "John, God must have sent the rain to quiet the water, for I asked him to help us." It was a very wet but thankful crowd that reached home that night.

In the spring that Bessie was fourteen years old, her father sold the beautiful home where she had spent so many happy days, and bought a tract of land in a dense wood farther up the lake. On account of the dense forest, the place appeared very dismal. As the purchaser of their old home wanted possession as soon as possible, Mr. Worthington had time to build only a barn before removing his family. In this building they lived during the first summer. Though these circumstances were discouraging, the Worthingtons tried hard to be brave. By fall a house was ready for them.

Many good things were lacking in this new forest home; but God knew this, and he put it into the hearts of friends and neighbors to supply the family with fruit and vegetables and also chickens. So generously were these supplied that there was no lack.

During the winter following much wood was cut, hauled, and piled out along the roadside in front of the house; but still there was standing timber nearly everywhere one might look, and to the south and west it extended for many miles.

The next summer Bessie learned how dangerous an enemy a large forest could become. There was so little rain during the hot months that things became dry and brittle. One day she heard the cry of "Fire! Fire!" Looking away to the southwest, she beheld a sight that made her feel faint with fear. The woods were ablaze, and the fire was coming directly toward her home.

Her father came to her, explained their danger, told her to warn her mother and then to do all she could to put out any sparks that might fall around the woodpiles, house, or barn. This said, he hastened to join the men in their desperate battle with the fire. When Bessie entered the house, she saw her mother weeping over her little baby, who had been born during the winter months and who had known nothing but sickness and suffering. When Mrs. Worthington heard the news, she continued to weep, and said, "Well, dear, do all you can to put out the sparks; for I think your little brother is dying, and I can not leave him."

By much hard work, the fire was held in check until evening. Bessie made her rounds with a pail of water and a dipper until her eyes became so painful on account of the smoke and heat that she was forced to lie down on the ground until they quit hurting. As soon as possible, however, she returned to her task, informing her mother frequently of the progress of the fire.

At last word came that nothing more could be done; that the house could not be saved. Seeing that further effort was useless and that each moment increased the danger of their own lives, the men left off fighting the fire, in order to save themselves and to help, if possible, the Worthington family. They soon reached the house. The next question was, where to go. The lake seemed to be the nearest place of safety. Confusion was everywhere, but through it all Mrs. Worthington sat quietly holding her dying baby.

"O Mama," said Bessie, "aren't you going with the rest?"

"No," answered her mother positively; "I shall remain right here with my dying child. I can not move him now and add to his suffering. I know that God can take care of me here as well as anywhere else. Why, Bessie, where is your faith? God can yet send rain and put out the fire."

"Oh! but if God doesn't send rain, you will burn up; for the fire is almost here," cried Bessie. "Do come as far from the house as you can, won't you?"

"No, Bessie, I told you, no. I shall sit just where I am," answered Mrs. Worthington; and Bessie knew that it would be useless to press the matter further.

With throbbing heart Bessie ran to her room, which was already getting hot from the fire: she fell upon her knees by the window where she could see the flames leaping from tree to tree, and began to call mightily upon God. "O God!" she prayed, "do send rain or change the wind." After repeating this prayer several times, she noticed some large drops of water upon the window pane. She knew what it meant: once before God had sent rain to help her in time of danger. Hastening down stairs, she said, "Mama, it's raining." "Thank God!" said Mrs. Worthington, "I knew he wouldn't let baby and me burn up."

By that time the rain was pouring down; the wind had ceased; and the danger was over. The rain did not put out the fire, but so checked it that, by hard work, it could be kept under control until it died out.

Little Clement lived only a short time after the fire; but just before he died, he looked into his weeping mother's face and smiled three times. As he had never smiled before, Mrs. Worthington always thought that God took that way to encourage her heart.

CHAPTER XIX.

LOST IN THE WOODS.

As Leroy was too young to drive the cows home in the evening, Bessie enjoyed many a long walk in search of them. One evening she had some difficulty in finding them. It was one of those evenings when everything is quiet and sound travels a long distance. After listening carefully for the tinkling of the cow-bells, Bessie was bewildered, for she could seemingly hear them in every direction. At last, thinking she had located the sound, she set out in that direction. When she had walked about two miles, she stopped to listen again. The bells were still tinkling, but they seemed to be just as far away. She knew, though, that the cows sometimes went a long distance. She had been following the road, but thinking the sound came from the woods, she started off in that direction. She saw that the sun was just going down behind the trees; that she was on an unfamiliar path, and was getting farther and farther from home. But she must get the cows, and on she went, stopping now and then to locate the sound of the bells.

She suddenly found herself standing upon a point of land where a deep, wide ravine extended on either side. The distance across the ravine she could not see on account of the shadow and the trees. What should she do? A few minutes previously she had thought about its being late, but had hoped to find the cows and to make them guide her home. This hope failing, she did not know what to do. The bells were still tinkling ahead of her; but she did not dare to try to cross the ravine in the darkness, now fast gathering around her, and how could she return through those dense woods! She thought of calling for help, but as quickly realized how useless the effort would be, since there were no houses near.

As she stood wondering what to do, these words from a psalm she had committed to memory a short time before, came to her mind: "If I say, Surely the darkness shall cover me; even the night shall be light about me. Yea, the darkness hideth not from thee; but the night shineth as the day; the darkness and the light are both alike to thee." Two more precious promises came to her mind: "I will guide thee with mine eye" and "He leadeth me beside still waters." Oh, what encouragement those words were to Bessie! Surely God would guide her home. With a thankful heart, Bessie started to return. As she had passed through several clearings in her search for the cows, she had no little difficulty in finding her way; but the moon rose early and gave her considerable light, and as she neared home, she began to recognize some familiar objects.

But, in the meantime, how were her parents feeling? The cows returned early and were milked. Mrs. Worthington wondered why Bessie did not come with them, but thought she might have been delayed and would come soon. She prepared supper; but when she got it ready, Bessie was still absent.

"What can be keeping Bessie tonight?" Mrs. Worthington said anxiously to her husband. "She should have come home an hour ago."

"Oh, I suppose she has stopped somewhere to play," said Mr. Worthington carelessly.

"No; I don't think so," replied his wife. "Bessie always tries to be prompt, and I'm afraid something has happened. If she doesn't come soon, you had better go to look for her."

"Well, wait until dark," said Mr. Worthington; "and, if she isn't here then, I'll get some men and we'll search in different directions. Did you notice which way she went!"

"No," answered his wife, "but I think she went east."

At dark Mr. Worthington started out with the searching party. Mrs. Worthington tried not to worry; but when nine o'clock passed and half-past nine came, she felt a great anxiety creeping into her heart. Many times she offered an earnest prayer for Bessie's protection. After putting Leroy to bed she stationed herself in front of the house to watch.

About ten o'clock some one returned to say that he could find no trace of Bessie.

With straining eyes, Mrs. Worthington looked in the direction in which Bessie had gone, and at last thought that she could see some one approaching. As the figure drew nearer, she could see that it was her child, and with a glad cry ran to meet her. "O Bessie," cried the mother, "what has happened to detain you? Your father and a company of men are out searching the woods for you. Dear child, where have you been?"

Bessie was very tired and hungry; but she related all that had happened and said: "I'm sorry I couldn't go farther; for I believe the cows were just a short distance beyond the point where I turned back. But I did not dare to cross the swampy place and go into the woods on the other side."

"Why, the cows have been home a long, long time, Bessie; and that is what had made your delay seem so strange," said her mother. "But were you not afraid, dear, when you found that you were so far from home!"

Bessie explained how she had felt and how the Lord had encouraged her and helped her to be brave.

"What time was that?" asked her mother; and when she learned, she said, "Bessie, that was when I was so earnestly praying for you. Surely our God is a mighty God and one who is ever faithful."

When the searching party returned, they were all glad to know that Bessie was safe at home.

CHAPTER XX.

NOVEL-READING.

As Bessie approached her sixteenth year, Mrs. Worthington became very anxious about her. The mother thought that she could notice a change in her daughter's actions and disposition. Instead of being confiding and happy, she seemed listless, forgetful, and nervous. At first the mother could not understand this change; but by close observation she found that her daughter was indulging in light reading.

Some magazines and weekly papers containing continued love-stories had found their way into the Worthington home. At first they were not attractive to Bessie. She would merely glance through the pages; but she gradually came to overlook the good, substantial reading and to enjoy the part that stimulated the romantic and imaginative part of her nature. The effect upon her mental and moral powers was much the same as that produced upon the digestive organs by rich and stimulating foods. Her mind was thus weakened and robbed of its relish for wholesome reading. She was ever looking forward for something to excite or satisfy her abnormal desire for the romantic or the dreadful.

As soon as Mrs. Worthington realized her daughter's danger, she sought an opportunity to instruct her on the dangers of novel-reading. "Some effects of novel-reading," said she, "are worse even than those produced by dancing. Many novels are hurtful because of the many false ideas interwoven in the stories. Some novels attract the pure-minded by their morality; but it is unsafe to read them, for the reason I have already given you, and because, as with any bad habit, the exciting influences must be constantly increased. In this way some persons are deceived and drawn into many of Satan's snares.

"In most novels there is much that is good and true; but the immoral, the worldly, and the untrue are so interwoven with it that the reader unconsciously finds himself taking pleasure in thoughts which, before he began reading novels, would have been disgusting. In this way the reader's sense of right is lowered and an appetite created—an appetite that can not be satisfied; the more it is fed, the more depraved and exacting it becomes. Gradually the desire for the romantic increases until the novel-reader longs to have a romance of her own. Her sense of duty is so blunted and her better judgment so blinded that she often agrees to a secret marriage with some one who is wholly unfit to be her life companion. It is in this way that many a girl has been deceived and led into sin. Many times, too, habits have been formed, from which nothing but the grace of God could deliver. In looking back over a wasted life, many a person can see that his or her downfall had its origin in the first novel.

"My dear child, there are many good books that you will find both helpful and interesting, but the Bible should be the pattern of your life. Let it be the principal food for your mind and soul. Your time all belongs to God, and you should waste none of it in reading unwholesome literature."

As Mrs. Worthington finished speaking, she was glad to see a changed look in Bessie's face. She knew that God was talking to her daughter; and as she arose to go, she said: "Bessie, do not forget from whom you may expect strength. I am praying that God will entirely take away the unnatural appetite which you have been fostering."

It was not long until Bessie rejoiced in full deliverance from her taste for novel-reading, and her interest in her mother's talks returned. As they read the Bible together and praised God for the precious truths it contained, cherishing them within their hearts as priceless treasures, Bessie's understanding seemed to open, and she was able to comprehend many of the deep truths of God's Word. The reading of God's Word gave her such unbounding joy, such complete spiritual happiness, that nothing could compare with it. Its truths, so simple and yet so grand, were at once a guide and a reproof to keep her feet from straying from the narrow way.

CHAPTER XXI.

GLAD TIDINGS.

In a small house about two miles from Bessie's home lived a very old lady. She loved the Lord and enjoyed telling of his goodness and of his dealings with her. Bessie, who was now about sixteen years of age, enjoyed these talks very much.

One day while Bessie and her mother were visiting this aged saint, she brought forth a much-worn paper and handed it to Mrs. Worthington, saying, "My daughter sent me this paper. You may take it home, if you like," she continued; "but I must ask you to return it, as my daughter wants it again." As Mrs. Worthington took the paper, Bessie saw at the top of the page, in large letters, "The Gospel Trumpet." After reading a few minutes Mrs. Worthington exclaimed: "This paper is certainly the work of a people who understand the plan of salvation. Things are fully explained here that have been plain to me for years—things that I dared not mention publicly lest I be thought fanatical."

On their return home Mrs. Worthington said: "It must have been in answer to prayer that Sister Moore let me see that paper. I have prayed for many years that God would help me to find a people who were not afraid to preach his whole Word. I believe we have found them. Who knows but this is God's way of starting a series of meetings here. Oh, the wonderful God we serve! I shall subscribe for the paper at once and also send my poem on sectism to see if they will publish it." The subscription was sent, and the poem soon appeared in the paper.

Mrs. Worthington was truly thankful to find that God had others in the world who were willing to teach the whole Bible without construing any part to suit their own ideas.

It was not long until a testimony appeared from a minister living a few miles away; and, agreeably with Mrs. Worthington's request, a series of meetings was started in the neighborhood.

CHAPTER XXII.

THE MEETINGS.

The news of the good meetings spread rapidly, and the attendance constantly increased. The gospel as preached was a new message to the people, and yet it was the very same that Jesus and his disciples taught. Every point of doctrine presented had a "thus saith the Lord" to confirm it.

Many saw that the Bible had been misunderstood and had been misconstrued by mankind to prove minor points, while the deep and vital truths had been so covered over with prejudice and unbelief that the majority of the people were blind to the true meaning of the Word; and that, in their confusion, each had gone to the denomination that seemed most nearly to correspond to his clouded views. It was also clearly shown that there is no way to heaven except the straight and narrow way that Jesus taught, and that God's Word is the only true measure of a Christian experience.

Mrs. Worthington felt now that her cup of joy was full since she could hear the way of salvation and the true church explained from the pulpit just as God had revealed them to her. She was also glad that Bessie, who was now old enough to understand deep spiritual truths for herself, was in perfect harmony and fellowship with her.

About forty souls were saved in the meetings; some gained the experience of sanctification; and the Spirit of the Lord worked mightily upon the hearts of many others.

Oh, the deep and wonderful love of God! Oh, the richness and fulness of his grace! How glorious Bessie now found her walk with God! How precious to commune with him and feel that she was growing deeper into his love! Truly it was a taste of heaven!

CHAPTER XXIII.

BESSIE SEES HER DUTY.

Among those converted in the meetings was a girl a little younger than Bessie. Her name was Cora. Being an orphan and living in the home of an infidel uncle, where she had no one to understand or sympathize with her views, she often sought Bessie for counsel and advice. The uncle did not oppose his niece, but others in his family did.

As time went on, the two girls became anxious to be doing something for the Lord. While they were pondering over the matter, a company of ministers came to the place to hold another series of meetings. From them the girls learned that *The Gospel Trumpet* was published by consecrated labor, that the workers received no stated salary, but that they trusted the Lord for their food and clothing.

It seemed a strange story to the girls, but Cora felt that she should like to go and help in the work. Though her uncle was not pleased with her plan, yet finally, after he had investigated and had found the place respectable, he gave his consent. It was several months, however, before she expected to leave. Toward the close of this time Bessie began to feel some anxiety for her friend, and one day said to her, "Cora, do you really want to go to *The Gospel Trumpet* office to work? Now, if you don't want to go, God will not be pleased with your service." "Bessie, I have lost all desire to go," Cora answered. "It seems to me that God is calling you instead of me. You could be a much greater help than I, because you have known and understood this truth all your life."

If Bessie had received a severe blow, it could not have hurt her more. Her precious mother! How could she leave her! Many of her cherished hopes for the future arose before me. Her plan, to do all she could for her mother in her declining years, came up before her; and as she thought of it, she became very sad. When the two girls parted at the door, Bessie's heart was very heavy; and when she was at last alone, she wept bitterly. She remembered that she had consecrated to do anything the Lord might require of her, but she did not see how she could do this. For many days Bessie bore this heavy burden; and, not being strong, she began to fail in health. From appearances, she had a malignant form of quick consumption. The course of the disease was rapid, and in a few weeks she was not only confined to her bed, but seemingly very near death. Mr. Worthington desired to consult a physician, but reluctantly heeded to Bessie's earnest entreaties to let her trust the Lord. She said to her father, "I know that God would heal me, if for the best; and, if not, I would rather die." And she added mentally, "I would rather die than to leave home."

Bessie at last became so low that she could not be left alone night or day. As her mother sat beside her one day, holding her hand, she said: "I believe, dear, that God wants to heal you and use you for himself. I feel like asking our elder, Sister Smith, to come and anoint you with oil according to Jas. 5:14, 15. I am sure God will heal you."

Sister Smith was brought as soon as possible; but, to Mrs. Worthington's surprise, she did not offer to anoint Bessie until the next day. She said: "I can not understand this case. There is something here that seems very strange. Bessie appears to be perfectly resigned to die, but she only answers yes or no to my questions. I shall talk to her again." Returning to the bedside, she said, "My dear, if God heals you, are you willing to leave your father, mother, and home to preach the gospel"—but she got no farther. Bessie, with all the emphasis she could command in her weak state, interrupted, "No; I will never preach."

"Ah! there is the point in your consecration that you have not reached," replied Sister Smith. "You must be willing to do anything that will bring the most honor to God's name, and to work where he can get the most glory out of your service. It may be the Lord will never require you to preach; but he wants the willingness on your part, just as much as if he wanted to make a minister of you."

It was some time before Bessie could answer; but when she did, it was to say that she would do anything, only that she must know that it was God who required it.

"God will make you to know that," said Sister Smith; "and now I feel that everything is out of the way, and we can ask God to heal you."

As she applied the oil and called earnestly upon God, there seemed to be a heavenly atmosphere filling the room. Bessie felt a soothing sensation passing through her body; and when the prayer was ended, she felt perfectly well, though exceedingly weak. Her strength soon returned, however, and it was not long until the Lord told her plainly that he wanted her at *The Gospel Trumpet* office. She remembered her consecration and felt willing in her heart to obey; but she shrank from telling her parents. For two weeks she endured severe mental suffering. She tried to gain sufficient courage to speak to her mother about the call, but her tongue refused to form the words. One day while she and her mother were in the cosy sitting-room, Mrs. Worthington said, "Bessie, I believe that God wants you at *The Gospel Trumpet* office and that he has used Cora's plan and your sickness to show you your duty."

Looking up through eyes filled with tears, Bessie related all that God had revealed to her. A great calm then came into her soul.

But the test was not entirely over. Mr. Worthington must be told, and—would he be willing? Embracing the first opportunity, Bessie told him her plans and begged his approval upon them; but his reply nearly crushed her.

"Bessie," said her father, "if you must leave us, you may go; but I have one thing to say and I mean it. If you go, you can never return; for your going is heartless indeed. I can not see why you should choose to go from your comfortable home and those who love you so dearly, and leave your mother, who so much needs your help."

"Father, Father!" exclaimed Bessie, "Oh, don't talk that way! You know how much I love you all. You know I never wanted to leave home before; and if you won't let me return, what shall I do?"

As she stood there before her father almost broken-hearted, a sweet voice whispered, "I will be with thee; be not afraid." The words sounded like music in her soul and reminded her of her recent decision to obey the Lord at any cost; and she said quietly:

"Well, Father, if you refuse to let me return home, it will have to be that way; but I must obey the Lord, and he has called me into his service"

"Very well," he answered, "but remember my words," and he left her.

Seeking her mother, Bessie told her of the interview and of her father's refusal to allow her to return home. For a moment they stood looking at one another; and then, with great tears filling her eyes, her mother said:

"Remember the words of Jesus, 'There is no man that hath left house, or parents, or brethren, or wife, or children, for the kingdom of God's sake, who shall not receive manifold more in this present time, and in the world to come life everlasting.' Dear, child, I know your dutiful nature, and how you long to obey your parents; but the Bible says to obey them in the Lord. When you have to choose whom you will serve, God or your parents, you must choose the Lord."

"I will obey God," said Bessie quietly; and she began at once to prepare to leave home.

When all was ready and the morning of departure had come, Mr. Worthington went out to prepare to take his daughter to the train. He had been very silent all the morning, but Bessie's heart was so full that she had taken little notice of his behavior. Oh, how she longed for his consent for her to return! Her mother gave her every encouraging word possible. At last they looked out and saw that the horse was ready. As Bessie picked up her last bundle, the door opened, and her father, stepping in quickly, caught her in his arms. "O my child," he sobbed, "will you forgive me and come back as soon as the Lord will let you? I didn't mean what I said; but it is so hard to give you up. If you need anything, write to me at once and let me know about it, won't you?" and he tenderly kissed her. Bessie's heart was filled with joy, and she said that he could expect her home just as soon as the Lord would let her come.

"Read 1 Cor. 10:13 and Jas. 1:12 just as soon as you have time, dear," whispered Mrs. Worthington in her daughter's ear as she kissed her again before she jumped into the buggy beside her father. Then they drove away from the home and the mother that were so dear to Bessie's heart.

Very few words were spoken on the way to town, and after a long ride Bessie found herself on the train. It all seemed like a terrible dream; but there was a sweet peace and quietness in her soul, and her father's loving words rang again and again in her ears.

CHAPTER XXIV.

REVERIE.

In the days that followed Bessie's arrival at the *Trumpet* office, she found many ways in which she could help spread the gospel. She found, too, that she could preach in a way that was not at all distasteful to her; for she could set up many lines of type to be used in printing the gospel message in the *Trumpet*, which was carrying light and truth into many homes and preaching to hungry souls. But oh, how often she thought of the dear ones at home and of how they were missing her!

One evening, when she sought her room and sat down beside the window, as she had so often done at home, she began to review her life. As the soft shadows gathered slowly about her, she seemed to be at home again close beside her mother's knee, listening to her tender, loving words of sympathy and advice. Bessie could now see what they had been worth to her. They not only had prepared her for a common sphere in life, but had given her a thorough understanding of God's great plan of salvation. As she recalled her mother's prayers and talks, she realized that, through them, she had many times escaped what other girls had ignorantly blundered into, and had been spared a great many of the bitter sorrows that come into the lives of girls not taught at their mother's knee. In her thankfulness, she offered a fervent prayer to her heavenly Father that many more earnest, noble, and prayerful mothers might be found to guide their children through the critical period of childhood.

After three months Bessie returned home for a short visit with her parents. Upon her arrival she not only found a loving and tender welcome, but also learned that both her parents had accepted her call as from God. After a happy visit of two weeks she returned to her work. With the blessing of God upon her labors, we shall here bid her good-by.

In conclusion, we wish to say that what she became was principally in answer to her faithful mother's prayers. Had she been left—as many girls are—without a mother's tender love and confidence, mingled with many earnest prayers, she would have fallen into temptations that she never knew. She had fully proved the worth of a praying mother.

CHAPTER XXV.

A PLEA TO MOTHERS.

Home as God intended it is built upon the corner-stone of virtue and prayer. It makes no difference how beautiful the house nor how grand its contents, if the mother is a woman who does not care for God or virtue, the corner-stone of that home is lacking. Such a home can not stand when trial and temptation enter.

A stream never rises above its source, nor a home above the ideals of its founders. No matter how humble the home, do not belittle its possibilities. Anything so sacred as home can command heaven's choicest and best blessings. The humblest cabin may contain that element which makes home the shrine of happiness and the temple of peace, and will cause it to send forth saints and heroes.

Oh that parents, especially mothers, could realize their influence in the home, their power to direct the young minds around them into the proper channel! Let us so educate and train the children that they will be able to get the greatest good from their natural endowment and that they may use it in such a manner as will bring the most glory to God. So train them and so live before them in the home that in after-years they will say with pleasure: "This precept was always taught me by my parents. Father and Mother's holy example has been a priceless birthright to me."

This is true parenthood. It should be the ideal in every home. By this I mean parents who realize their responsibility and have their children's best interest at heart; parents who will sacrifice any pleasure of their own for the benefit and happiness of their little ones; parents who will not only bid their children a hearty welcome into the world, but will care for their future from that moment, and who have the love and respect of their entire household.

You may say that parents like these are few and hard to find. True, but it is equally so that, with proper knowledge and understanding, many would approach this standard. Perhaps some have allowed years to slip carelessly by and their darlings to pass seemingly beyond their control. To such I would say, It is never too late to pray.

Observe the wayward boy whose chief inheritance is a wild, wilful nature. He is nearing his fourteenth birthday. Having been allowed to have his own way while small, he has cultivated an ungovernable desire to do as he pleases. Let the mother of that boy cease her old habit of saying, "I don't know what will become of that boy! I don't understand how he can treat me so rudely. I've done all I can, and he just grows worse," and take a more rational method.

Have you gone to that boy and told him the sweet, simple story of Jesus and why he came from his beautiful home; that a part of his mission was to teach you how to make your home after the pattern of his heavenly home; that his heart is touched with compassion when he beholds any one in trouble; that he is grieved because you have made a mistake; but that you are sorry and are decided to do your duty? Have you told the boy all that? Have you knelt beside his bed at night with your tear-dimmed eyes pressed upon his hand, and told him the great dangers that are before him, even surrounding him, and informed him how to avoid them? Have you told him that he is at the most critical time in his life, that a mistake now will mean a life of suffering for both him and you, and that he can with you begin over and remove some of his past mistakes? Have you talked thus to your boy? If not, why not? It is your privilege as well as your duty.

CHAPTER XXVI.

PARENTAL DUTY.

The first duty of father and mother to their child is to see that they are a unit on family government. Second, they must study themselves and their failures, trying to make the weak places strong. Third, study the disposition of the child, gain an understanding of its inner life, and find out what pleases and displeases it; and, while cultivating the good, hold in check the bad. A mother should understand her children better than any one else. If she is a thoughtful mother, she knows not only the surroundings of her children, but many of the impressions that she has stamped upon their undeveloped minds.

Children are not putty that can be moulded into any form to suit our fancy, but there is a method by which we can fashion their young lives. Much patience, devotion to the child, and fervent prayer will be needful to accomplish anything worth while.

Every parent should see that their attitude toward their children is what it should be. Consider their feelings and show them respect, remembering that they have rights upon which you must not intrude; but never loosen the reigns of home government. Make any rules that you think practicable and necessary; explain each rule carefully to your child, giving your reason for making it, and then demand obedience. Never, unless for some special reason, ignore any good rule. Should your child happen to break one of these rules, do not punish without first finding out the cause. He may not have understood your meaning, or he may have forgotten. Take him quietly aside; and, after finding out why he has disobeyed, gently tell him again your reasons for making the rules and the necessity of his obedience. You might have to do this several times, but do not excuse him too long. When it is necessary to punish, ask for wisdom from above, and then punish in a way that he will understand you and remember the punishment. When you make a statement, stand by it, if possible, unless you see error in it. If such be the case, confess your fault. If your child does not show you due respect and obedience, there is a cause for it, and it is your duty to find out what that cause is.

All children have to contend with bad qualities that have been inherited. Do not flatter yourself that because the child is yours it will escape temptation; for all must be tempted, if they would be strong. Teach your children, according to their ability to comprehend, all that they should know to be able to shun evil. Do not think that because your child has inherited some moral weakness, you are helpless to teach him to overcome it. You can explain to him his danger and tell him what yielding to the temptations that come to him because of this weakness will lead to. Point out the effect of this sin upon the one from whom it was inherited. Tell the child that the only chance to overcome this inherited tendency will be by constantly avoiding those things that will lead to temptation. You may find the task difficult and you may sometimes feel disheartened, but you must put that wayward child of yours right, if possible, or God will hold you accountable. Perhaps the inherited sin may lie at your own door. If it does, you will understand better how to help him from under its power.

In the public school, on the street, and in his various associations, your child will be exposed to the evil of hearing impure language from vile lips; and if he be not warned, who can blame him for listening? Your home teaching must overbalance all that he hears outside.

Should some question concerning the mysteries of his own body or of his own origin be aroused in his mind by impure stories or by any other cause, you must at once arise to meet the difficulty before harm is done that will be very difficult to overcome. But some mother will say: "I do not know what answer to make my child when he asks questions of such a delicate nature. Would it not be best to leave his mind free from these ideas until he is older?" Doubtless it would, if the child would be contented to wait; but when he has learned enough to ask the question, he is able to tell whether you speak the truth when you say you do not know, and he will not be satisfied by the flimsy pretest, "Oh, run away and don't bother me; I'm too busy."

Above all else, keep the confidence of your child, so that he will come to you with every trouble of life. Confidence of children in their parents is a gift from God. All children have it at first. See the tottering baby cling to its mother for support; watch it run to her when it is frightened. Can it not have the same confidence when it is older? I answer from experience that it can and should. Truth inspires trust in your child. If you do not think it best to answer all his questions fully at the time when he asks them, tell him at least enough to satisfy his curiosity, and promise him that, if this remains a secret between you and him, he may come to you whenever he wants more information. Do not be afraid of having secrets with your child. The matter may be trifling, but the fact that he is helping you to keep secrets will teach him to value his word and will increase his confidence in you. On the other hand, if you tell him an untruth, do not think that he will come to you again. No, he will doubtless go to some friend who he thinks will tell him, and thus get his young mind tainted with impure thoughts. And little better in results than telling an untruth is putting the child off till some future time. These questions must be met when they arrive.

You may say, "I don't know how much to tell at any one time." Wisdom is necessary here. No more should be told than will satisfy the present curiosity of the child. A few questions on your part will readily discover what information he has gained and how much he wishes to know.

A boy of scarce six summers once came to his mother with a question of life. The mother was shocked; but, offering an earnest prayer for wisdom, she questioned the child and found that he had heard remarks made by older boys. As his mind was developed enough to comprehend part of their conversation, his curiosity was aroused. Having perfect confidence in his mother, he had sought her for an explanation of the points that perplexed him. As simply as possible, that mother gave the information, ending with the words, "Now, darling, this is to be a perfect secret between us; and when you are old enough, I will tell you more." Years passed by until the boy was in his eleventh year; then he once more went to his mother for information. "Mama," he began, "do you remember the time you told me a secret?" She answered that she did, and he continued: "Well, I have kept that secret. I have never mentioned it to any one. And do you remember that you said some time you would tell me more?" When she answered, "Yes," he said quickly, "Don't you think I'm old enough now?" In answer, the mother put her arms about him and said, "My son, you shall hear all you wish to hear. What is it, dear?" Then as each question came, she gave him a satisfactory answer, and ended by saying, "Whenever you want to know more, come to me, and I will tell you." That boy continued to go to his mother; and when he entered the most trying period of his life, her advice kept him from the dangers into which so many fall. In hours of trial she was able to point him to the Savior. Never neglect the duty of warning your child of danger.

Teaching of this kind will endear you to your children long after you are resting in the grave. They will recount, "My mother told me this. My father taught me that. They must have understood God's plan of salvation, or they would never have known how to tell me these things." But the task will require your highest talents. Sympathy and love, constant watchfulness, and earnest prayer will be the most needful. Since the child does not know himself, you must learn to know him. You must search for the secret springs that govern his actions and for the master key that will unlock his heart.

One dear young woman, relating her experience to me, said: "My mother died when I was only six years old; but I know she must have been a Christian, because some friends who knew her told me of her devoted life and of earnest pleadings for her children when she saw that she must leave them. All that I can remember about her was seeing her bowing in prayer or talking to us children. There are desires in my nature that I know must have been planted within me in answer to her prayer. After her death I was cast out upon the world. I went to live with a very ungodly family, but that sense of right and wrong within me made me shun and despise their evil ways. I loved to read my Bible. From it I learned that, if I would gain heaven, I must forsake sin and live a pure life. To live such a life was a pleasure until I found that the denomination whose meetings I attended would not allow me to say much about a holy life, because their creed did not teach it. Then I promised the Lord that I would be a Christian if I had to be one all by myself. This was not necessary, for I found many true Christians who believed all that the Bible teaches."

That mother's prayers had fashioned and governed the life of her daughter long before the child was able to understand her mother's meaning. Parents can not begin too early to win the child's love and confidence, and they should spare no pains to maintain these to mature years. Those who do will find that their children will never, even to old age, fail to come to them for sympathy and advice. Children so reared will always love and honor their father and mother as the Bible says they should, and will look upon their parents' lives as examples for them to imitate. See to it that you show yourself a good pattern, in thought, word, and deed, for them to follow.

CHAPTER XXVII.

USEFUL HINTS.

There is no definite rule whereby parents may control their home, except to seek advice from God, for no two families have the same environment. Any method that will bring about the desired result may be applied; but the method must be systematic and thorough. A positive attitude is good, and should be encouraged, but harshness ought never to be used. The latter will tend to discouragement and resentment in the child, while the former will teach the difference between right and wrong.

Be charitable to your children in regard to their faults and failings, so that they may learn by your example to be charitable to each other and to their fellows. Teach them the blessings that charity will bring to them; show them that it is the greatest of God's gifts and that without it they will meet many buffetings from their contact with the world. Remember that Paul speaks of it as "the more excellent way" and admonishes us to desire it above all things else.

Children must have entertainment. Rich and costly furniture, elaborate parties, or even guests are not necessary. Children may be entertained in a very simple manner. What child does not enjoy the old-fashioned game of hide-and-seek, tag, or some such innocent amusement with Papa and Mama? It may take a little of your time, but what of that? Do all you can to make your home the happiest place on earth for your children.

"Yes," says one, "that will do while the children are little; but just wait until they grow up, and then they will seek other company." I did not say that they must always stay with you. Of course they will desire to go from home sometimes. What I mean is that we can make home so attractive that they will note the difference between it and the outside world. The interest we take in them will constrain them to remain at home and to return when away from it. Home! Oh that beautiful word! Poets have written about it, choirs have sung about it, but who can fathom the meaning of that little word, home! None but the child who has been taught to revere, cherish, and enjoy it, and then looking back remembers the happy years spent in the home circle.

I think that I hear a father say, "When I return from my work, I am so tired I can not stand the children's noise." Is that so? Do you not love your children, and are you not working for their welfare! If so, do you not think that a little less labor with your hands and a little time spent with them would be more profitable? Perhaps a little romp or chat with them would rest you.

Try it anyway. You who are desk workers can afford it: it will help you to cast off the responsibilities of the day and the better prepare you for the morrow. A romp with the children is not lost; but, on the other hand, is a benefit for both parent and child. Thoughtful parents can think of many things that will increase the interest in home and will draw them closer to their children.

Sometimes it is good for the children to visit their friends, but parents should always be acquainted with these friends. Never let your child go where games are played that you would not allow played in your own home. Here is where conscience and confidence will help you. Be cautious about allowing your child to go somewhere to stay all night. In this way many a child has learned evil practises and in some cases been ruined. Then, too, it draws his mind away from the home circle.

"But," you say, "all this I have done, and yet my children are now forgetful of it all. They are indulging in many things that they were taught to be harmful to the soul." My dear friend, can you not remember when this state of things began? Can you not point to a time when there was a drifting from your home circle? when home life began to seem too narrow for your child? when he began to crave the association of others more than that of his own brothers and sisters? Did you at that time lift up your home banner and shield? Did you tell him of the rapids in the distance? "No," you falteringly answer; "I thought there could be no harm in allowing him to mingle with his chums at school and to visit them in their homes. I was afraid to be too particular, lest he should think me too strict with him." Ah! friend, that was your golden opportunity, and you failed to see it. After instructing the child, you should have bowed with him in prayer, giving him over to God's keeping. Then, if he chose to go—remembering that your prayers were following him—nine chances out of ten he would have returned with words similar to those spoken by a youth who had been permitted to attend a party. In answer to his father's question he said, "Yes; I had a good time, but I have better times at home." "Better times at home!" Think of it, parents! Is it not worth some self-denial, some sacrifices, on pour part, to have your home spoken of in this manner?

"Yes," says a mother, "that is all right when both parents are in harmony and have salvation; but suppose that the parents are poor and that one is unsaved?" I have seen just such homes as this governed in the manner whereof I speak. God gave more grace and strength to the saved companion; and, although there were many difficulties to encounter, yet the saved one was able to influence the home for God. "All things are possible to him that believeth," said Christ in olden times, and his statement is still true.

Again, I hear a parent whose loved companion has recently died say, "What can I do now to train my children aright?" There comes before my mind a beautiful scene of a faithful mother with her son and daughter whom she had brought up to God's glory. She was left alone with these two precious ones to guide and rear to manhood and womanhood. She bade adieu to the words "I can't" and with determination went about her task. As God never lets such zeal go without assistance, this mother found help in time of need. Another scene which I love to recall is that of a devoted father and by his side his two motherless daughters just entering womanhood. He gives them every spare moment that he has, and both are real examples of trust and purity.

In your zeal to find entertainment for your children, do not forget that they must have employment. See that every member of your household has certain work to do. This work should be suited to the years and the strength of the individual and, if possible, to his likes and dislikes. Work of the proper kind will strengthen the muscles, improve the health, keep out many evils, and create in the young a desire to help bear the burdens of life. Periods of rest may be made profitable by having on hand as much wholesome literature as you are able to secure. By this means much useful knowledge may be stored. The reading need not be confined wholly to religious works; reliable treatises on science, art, mechanics, cooking, chemistry, domestic economy, health, etc., are all profitable if not indulged in to the exclusion of religious literature. If you trust God, he will help you to know what to do.

A lady once said, "Our children are what we make them, and we get out of them just what we put in." These words contain much truth. God holds all parents, according to their light and understanding, responsible for the training of their children.

If you have a preference among your children, never reveal it. On the contrary, endeavor to place the less favored ahead in your care and attention. You can justly do this, for the favorite will get all the attention he deserves anyway. I well remember a case where the mother's favorite son brought sorrow and shame to the entire household by stealing from his own father, simply because she had humored and petted him in childhood. Parents can not be too careful in this respect.

Many a mother does not realize how highly her children value her opinion. A boy had met with an accident that somewhat disfigured him for a time. While he was preparing to leave for school, his mother said, "You will no doubt be made sport of today; are you able to bear it?" His answer was, "Oh, I don't care what any one says about me but you; but if you were to make fun of me, I couldn't stand it."

SWEET GEM OF THE HOME.

Thou formal home, so graced, so blest,
With earthly treasures rare;
Within thy portals we expect
All graces rich and fair.

We gaze, we search, but all in vain;
The gem we love so well,
"Sweet innocence," doth not remain,
Nor in thy chambers dwell.

Thy children, as the world they greet,
Are bearing tales of thee;
"I was not warned," they oft repeat,
Nor taught at Mother's knee.

Sweet Innocence, thou heav'nly grace,
Rich gem from God above!
Thy touch upon the human face
Reveals but peace and love.

Thy treasures richer far than gold,
Thy gifts of greatest worth,
Might grace our homes, except for sin,
Whose curse now sweeps the earth.

We look for thee within the maid,
With beauty, grace, and charm,
But find thy flight she hath not stayed,
Nor doth she feel alarm.

Then in the lad, whose noble brow
Thy presence might suggest;

With closer view we must allow
By thee he is not blest.

E'en when we look within the child
And laud his graces sweet,
We find his mind so soon defiled
For thee 'tis no retreat.

"And why?" we ask, "oh! why is this?
Such need and dearth abound.
Oh! why in homes of promised bliss
May not this gem be found?"

The mystery, so deep, so great,
Is simply lack of prayer;
Is bidding timely warning wait
For daily toil and care.

Allowing things that crumble, waste,
Our whole attention claim,
We cause sweet Innocence in haste
To leave our homes to shame.

But thee, sweet grace, we find in some—
Thank God thou art not lost!—
We see thee in the Christian home
As royal guest and host.

We note the mother as she pleads
For counsel from God's throne,
Then goes with wisdom that she needs
And strength to make it known.

We watch the child in this true home,

And in its face so fair
We recognise what doth become
A faithful mother's prayer.

Sweet Innocence! may we extol,
Within the home, thy art;
Thy power to beautify the soul,
To teach the pure in heart.

Thou gift divine! thou fairest gem!
Thy presence may we crave,
That thou mayst grace our diadem
In life beyond the grave.

Reveal, O grace, unto the world
Thy beauties rich and rare,
That all may understand and know
What mothers find in prayer.

Milton Keynes UK
Ingram Content Group UK Ltd.
UKHW030743071024
449371UK00006B/604